Ma Speaks Up

2018
For Michael

Ma Speaks Up

AND A FIRST-GENERATION DAUGHTER TALKS BACK

So delighted to know you!

Marianne Leone

Best

May—

BEACON PRESS
BOSTON

Beacon Press
Boston, Massachusetts
www.beacon.org

Beacon Press books
are published under the auspices of
the Unitarian Universalist Association of Congregations.

20 19 18 17   8 7 6 5 4 3 2 1

This book is printed on acid-free paper that meets the uncoated paper
ANSI/NISO specifications for permanence as revised in 1992.

Text design and composition by Kim Arney

Library of Congress Cataloging-in-Publication Data
Names: Leone, Marianne author.
Title: Ma speaks up : and a first-generation daughter talks back /
    Marianne Leone.
Description: Boston : Beacon Press, 2017.
Identifiers: LCCN 2016042279 (print) | LCCN 2017003480 (ebook) |
    ISBN 9780807060049 (hardback) | ISBN 9780807060056 (e-book)
Subjects: LCSH: Leone, Marianne. | Mothers and daughters—United
    States—Biography. | BISAC: BIOGRAPHY & AUTOBIOGRAPHY /
    Personal Memoirs. | FAMILY & RELATIONSHIPS / Parenting /
    Motherhood.
Classification: LCC CT275.L3676 A3 2017 (print) | LCC CT275.L3676
    (ebook) | DDC 306.874/3092 [B] —dc23
LC record available at https://lccn.loc.gov/2016042279

For my brother and sister,
all of us from the same source,
and each of us with a different tale to tell

Prologue
Argument with Myself

Last night my elderly mother knocked over the television set in my living room with a deliberate sweep of her once powerful arms, all the while glaring at me. I was amazed at her old-age strength and riveted by her eyes, windows to a soul on fire. Then she collapsed in my overstuffed chair, shivering, whimpering piteously that she was cold even after I sat down and wrapped my arms around her. She felt like a shrunken husk. I couldn't comfort her, and as I pressed her more closely to me, she disappeared. This was a dream, although when my mother was in her thirties she would have been perfectly capable of knocking over a television set, or possibly lifting a car if my brother were trapped under it. She once put her fist through a door in one of her rages.

I take the dream as a sign of her displeasure with my plan to write about her life and to tell the unvarnished truth. She asked me to "tell her story." I know she would rather I write a gooey-centered bonbon of a daughter-love book, scored with Connie Francis cry-singing "Mamma," with a light dusting of pity scattered over it like confectioners' sugar. But that's not the truth. The truth is,

I was a merciless daughter until the last ten or so years of her life, seizing on her every flaw, mocking her English, skeeving her touch. I was the cuckoo in the nest, the unnatural changeling who didn't even cry when separated from her on the first day of kindergarten, the ingrate who spurned her every gift. "You no belong to this family!" she would scream at me, spittle flying. I would *Deo gratias* my response, sickening inside although outwardly I wore a smirk, like every bully. Who wants to hear this mother-daughter shit? Other, better writers have covered the dysfunctional mother–damaged-daughter nexus. But my mother wasn't dysfunctional. She was just foreign, from another country, another time, another world. She couldn't be my mother, this alien, this *immigrant*. I read books. She hated books. I loved words. She fought furiously, hopelessly with the English language, losing every round, retiring into defeated, bitter silence in her corner while I performed a jeering victory dance in mine, fists raised triumphantly, oblivious to my own privilege. She wanted to enfold, to care for the child that was finally hers and hers alone. But every photo of me from the time I could stand shows a stick-limbed child moving away from her, scrabbling out of her arms, fighting to hold onto myself so she couldn't engulf me in a molasses tidal wave, knocking me over, stealing my breath, drowning me in a flash flood of her sticky love.

I don't think this is the book she would have wanted. But maybe, just maybe, she would have laughed in recognition of some of the truths here. And perhaps that dream wasn't a gloomy portent; it might have been describing the birth process. I was cold, too, after giving birth. I know what that feels like. I know what it's like to shrink and disappear. I couldn't hold my own child close enough, ever. All I wanted was to disappear into my son, into my own tidal wave of love. And after I lost him, after I found him dead in his bed on a morning in January, I wanted my mother. But she had died six months before my son.

I'm no longer running away from her. I'm trying to bring her back in the only way I can, by diving deep into the murky, emotion-clouded memories of her and by letting Ma speak up, so I can tell her story, and talk back to her here, on the page, safe from flying kitchen implements and ready at last for her embrace.

The Official Story

The young girl crouches, listening to the men decide her fate. She is as still as a woodland creature, hidden among the goats in the barn that is attached to her whitewashed stone house on the outskirts of Sulmona, at the foot of the fearsome Apennines. The oil lamp in the primitive kitchen gives a falsely cheery glow, one that belies the grimness of the talk within. Her father offers two pigs and five hectares of land. The hunchback laughs and shakes his head. He knows that he is the solitary bidder for this skinny girl. Il Duce— Benito Mussolini—has promised a bounty for sons; this rag looks unlikely to be the mother of future soldiers. Even in the gloom, the girl can see the hunchback's blackened teeth, his twisted back. He is old, older than her father. His sour smell rises above the pungent odor of the goats who mutter and shift beside her, their devil eyes like his, the *gobbo*, the hunchback who will take her to his bed.

She hates her father. He is cruel, his green eyes glinting with spite. Her mother sleeps in the girl's narrow bed with her at night. Sometimes her father comes home drunk, his short, thick body knocking into things, and then he grows into a towering colossus, a monster inflated by the rough talk at the café in the piazza. He strikes her mother, calls her *puttana*, tries to pull her from the young girl's bed. He is a man who deserves respect, the head of the house. Her father is a fascist; he lives by Mussolini's words: Believe! Obey! Fight! But his wife fights him; she spits in his face. The young girl knows what to do: she runs to find her mother's father, her *nonno*, who will come with the gun, the gun that kills the wolves that come down from the mountains at night to cull the herd of sheep. Her father is a wolf; he has no pity. He devours his prey. She and her mother are prey.

And now the girl will be separated from her mother and go to live with the *gobbo* in his filthy lair, like a princess sacrificed to a dark god. But the very next day her mother appears, glowing like the *befana* at Epiphany and gives the girl a precious gift: her freedom. The mother tells the girl she will send her to L'America, where she will marry when and if she pleases, for love; she will not be a token for pigs or hectares of land. The girl herself will choose. She will live with the mother's sister in the absurd-sounding state of Massachusetts where she will have a future and be safe in a place where the coming of war does not thud with the dull certainty of a hoe cracking the starved earth. She will know kindness; she will be granted mercy. She will be happy.

On the boat crossing, the girl worries her meager treasures like rosary beads: the stark photograph of her unhappy mother, the picture frame made of sugared almonds, the dried flower, a secret token from the boy she wanted but could not have. She is dressed in many layers of clothes to save space in her bundle and to give the illusion of robust good health to the officials who guard the gates to L'America. She allows herself to dream, to hope for happiness.

The girl suffers a purgatory of years in the New World. The aunt puts her to work in the garment district of Boston mere days after her arrival. She sews all day long with people who can't pronounce her name and who speak amongst themselves in a harsh, clacking tongue. She receives a new name, an American one that slightly resembles her own and makes her feel like a changeling. She gets lost in the maze of Boston and stands crying in the dirty streets. Her aunt's adopted son resents her, the interloper. The girl is sent to live with strangers. Six months after she arrives in this cacophonous, unfriendly place she receives word that her mother is dead. Her father remarries less than a year later, a disgrace. Now her yearnings for the lonely farmhouse are tempered with the understanding that return is impossible. There is no home, just a space on a strange family's sofa where she hears them whispering about her at night.

Then, a glimmer of light. Her aunt opens a store in an Italian neighborhood outside of Boston. The girl works at the small, cramped store, selling notions and yarn, and makes a friend, a teenage girl who speaks her language. The joy of giggling in her mother tongue with someone her own age! For the first time since coming to L'America, she doesn't cry at night. She is invited to the teenager's house, a wonderland of laughter and savory food. She is enfolded, entranced by this new family, so unlike her own. The mother is short and round and pretty. She makes jokes and her children adore her. The father is shy and gruff in the way of country people, but welcoming. There is a handsome older brother, a young man whose generous nature is glazed over with sorrow. The girl sees only his smile, his thick, wavy hair, the elegant clothes. Within two weeks, there is a pact. They marry, because the young man needs to settle down and the girl is young and innocent and from the old country. Love comes later, overcoming gratitude, and the girl is at last happy.

This was my mother. That was my father. This is the official story.

And like all immigrant stories, it's not the whole story, and it's only partly true.

Aunt Ellie, my father's younger sister, was the storyteller in our family. Ellie had exciting tales about the dating buffet that was Boston during World War II, the handsome men in various uniforms that took her to dances and movies, the time she made a date with two guys for the same night and sent my safely married mother to suss out which one was cuter, the boy who took her to a graveyard to make out, thinking she'd be scared and let him get to second base. She sat at our kitchen table with the red enamel top and silver sides, a conjurer wreathed in smoke, filling ashtrays, telling her tales. Ellie talked about the tough times, too, during the Depression, when they almost lost the house the family had scraped and sacrificed to buy. They had to rent out the downstairs and cram themselves into the four upstairs rooms, making do, washing dishes in the bathtub. Ellie contributed by ironing clothes for rich people. She was only twelve years old, but what she earned helped pay the electric bill. She spoke of the pride she felt walking the two miles to Watertown Square from the family home in Newton, the ironing money clutched tightly in her hand, and the gratification she felt knowing she was helping to keep the house from foreclosure by the always looming bank. There were glamorous pictures of Ellie as a young woman, long-legged and red-lipped, in a fur coat, auburn Rita Hayworth hair spilling over her shoulders, or sitting with a handsome serviceman, dressed in something slinky, a cocktail on the table before her. An oval-framed portrait showed a younger Ellie on the day of her Holy Communion, a miniature bride in a long white dress and veil. A tinted family picture portrayed her at four, innocent in a smocked dress, leaning shyly against her proud mother.

There were no pictures of my mother as a teenager or as a child.

My mother doled out information about her past in grudging non sequiturs that made no sense in the worldview of my early sixties American childhood. Ellie's stories made me love her. My mother's stories left me puzzled and sometimes afraid. Her one-liners were like ominous messages discovered on an ancient tablet from a lost civilization. The truncated anecdotes were non-sensical and scary and even funny in a macabre kind of way. Once I pointed to a faint scar over her left eyebrow and she told me that a donkey had kicked her in the head when she was around my age (ten at the time). I didn't know any other kids whose mothers had been kicked in the head by a donkey. Nor did any of my friends have a mother who had marched for Il Duce. In my early twenties, I took her to see *A Special Day*, a Sophia Loren-Marcello Mastroianni film about fascist Italy. My mother shouted in delighted recognition upon seeing the kids dressed in their Balilla uniforms—"That was me! I march for Il Duce!" My mother the fascist, I thought, with a kind of sour wonder, as I shushed her, looking around the darkened theater, afraid someone had heard. My mother had no entertaining stories about dating different guys like Aunt Ellie did, only dark tales about arranged marriages and oblique references to the unhappy one between her own mother and father. Neither did she have any wedding pictures.

I was obsessed with wedding portraits when I was a kid. In the early sixties, it was my destiny, my certain future, and the glowing endgame scenario—to be a bride. My father talked about "walking me down the aisle" someday, his chest already puffed at the thought. My childhood friends played bride and planned their elaborate weddings. I was a flower girl at cousins' weddings, strewing blossoms down the aisle, my future path to glory. I received bride dolls for Christmas, stiff blinking mannequins swathed in lace that were meant more as symbolic totems to be venerated than actual playthings. Both sets of aunts and uncles had elegant black-and-white wedding photographs, the aunts in satin dresses with trains that pooled around their feet, flowing like quicksilver. My aunt Ellie's sister-in-law, Camille, who lived downstairs, had a thick cream-colored leather album of black-and-white photographs documenting the connubial rites, from the first ceremonial laying on of the lacy white veil in her bedroom to the hammy end photo of the bride and groom waving good-bye in the decorated getaway car. I had memorized the details of every picture and handled the album like a sacred text. Whenever I slept over, I headed straight for that book, perched in a place of honor atop a white doily, while my aunt and her sister-in-law had their morning coffee break and daily rehash of local gossip and yesterday's soaps.

The nuns at Our Lady Help of Christians, where I went to school, taught us that marriage was a sacrament. A marriage was only valid if sanctioned by a priest who performed the sacred rite in a church. Where was the picture of my mother and father happily exiting the church under a hail of rice with the priest blessing them at the door? Where was the staged portrait of my mother, her bashful eyes cast down, clad in the creamy satin gown, the veil dripping with hand-tatted lace, the white signifying her virginal, untouched state? This lack of documentation troubled me most of all because it involved God. I had a horrible feeling that the missing photograph was a sin of omission that meant my parents were not in God's good graces, and that by some awful blood contagion I wasn't, either. Our family was possibly cursed, with hell yawning before us. I might even be a bastard child or some other sort of unofficial non-person. Where was the proof my mother and father were married in the eyes of the church? Was our family legit? Could God even see us?

I asked my mother these questions over and over, with the inhuman persistence of an interrogator at a black ops site. Her replies were usually distracted half-truths that were ludicrously inadequate excuses to a Nancy Drew buff like me. For instance, she tried to pass off a posed photograph of herself in what was obviously a bridesmaid's dress as her wedding portrait. How could she think that I, a junior matrimonial connoisseur, could be fooled by such a blatant untruth? Really? Where was her veil? It couldn't possibly have been that voile bonnet that tied under her chin. Even in black and white you could tell the non-wedding veil was pastel colored. Unheard of! Sometimes the relentless inquiries would trigger my mother's volcanic temper and I would crouch under the eruption of her anger with my questions unanswered, afraid to move, frozen like those filled-in statues at Pompeii, ineffectively dodging the fiery ash that doomed them forever.

My mother could be chatty on topics unrelated to weddings, but her ramblings were bizarre and somehow irritating tales that were as zany and outlandish as Saturday morning cartoons. When I was around twelve she looked up from my latest report card and told me that she was always the first one to raise her hand in school and volunteer to go down to the river and wash the teacher's clothes. Once I got over picturing myself scrubbing Sister Eudes's mysterious underwear in the scummy waters of the Charles River at the end of my street, I took this information as a passive/aggressive slur on my smarty-pants straight-A grades, since I didn't have the first clue how to operate our washing machine, a skill my mother would have admired much more than my consistently stellar grades. One day I asked about my grandmothers, both dead before I was born. She shocked me by saying:

"My mother didn't love my father. She was going to run away with someone else."

Before I could digest this drama, she topped herself by telling me she was born in this country, in Watertown, just a few miles from where we lived now. She said that her mother and father had come here to make a new life. But her father had discovered my grandmother's affair and "ripped up the passports," in my mother's words. The unhappy couple, along with my newborn mother, returned home to Abruzzi, where my mother grew up with no memory of the United States or knowledge that she was an American citizen.

While my head still swam with the news that my mother was actually American, she launched into a story about my other grandmother, a story that was really about my mother herself. She told me about the day she brought coffee up to her mother-in-law's bedroom, where she lay, invalided by heart disease. My mother, newly wedded to my father, served coffee and sweets to all her mother-in-law's friends, but after they left, my grandmother told my mother, "You should've put poison in their coffee. They all talked bad about you." I was confused. "But why?" I asked my mother. "Why? Why would they say mean things about you?" She shrugged. End of story. Was it because she didn't have a wedding picture? But I knew if I asked that question, I would trigger an eruption; I could tell by the way she pulled down her mouth and looked away. I remained adrift in a sea of family half-truths, confused and resentful at the cruel irony that my American-born mother didn't seem in the least American. There was nothing open or guileless or hopeful or optimistic about her. Ma was as murky and baleful as a sibyl at Cumae. Nothing about my family made sense.

When I became a teenager, the entire Mystery of the Missing Wedding Picture became as insignificant to me as the Nancy Drew books gathering dust in my bookcase. I no longer cared about my mother's past, and I didn't worry about whether or not my parents had been married in the Catholic Church. "Keep your rosaries off my ovaries," I chanted with other feminists as we marched through Boston defying the patriarchy. I renounced the church and the directives of the old men in dresses giving orders from Rome. I would never get married, I decided. I would never dress up like a bride doll and walk down the aisle of some church to be "given away" by my father. He couldn't give me away, anyway, because he was dead, at fifty, and my young mother, now widowed with three children and no way to make a living, had to apply survival skills dormant for the twenty-two years she was married to my father. We declared a mother-daughter truce and sheathed our rapiers, too busy now to indulge in the luxury of squabbling, exchanging the daily verbal death of a thousand cuts for grieving my father and the grim but necessary pursuit of food and shelter.

When I became an adult the struggles eased and my mother made me laugh more often than she made me angry. Ma's worried overprotection during my coddled childhood had only served to distance us. I could never picture her hardscrabble beginnings and she resented the self-absorbed child she had helped to create. She kept her secrets, as befitted someone raised in the inaccessible, shrouded mountains; I over-shared, like all the sunny American children of my pig-in-the-python generation. My own mellowing came right on schedule after I became a mother, too, and had been married happily for a number of years. As it turned out, I didn't have a formal wedding portrait either, just a snapshot in a vintage wedding dress that was a seventy-five-dollar find from a jumped-up antique shop on Forty-Third Street in Manhattan. The irony of the non-wedding dress worn by a former wedding-obsessive was not lost on me. *Sic transit gloria mundi.*

Years later, I sat across from Aunt Ellie at her laminated faux-maple table smoking a Benson & Hedges bummed from her ever-present open pack. In her late seventies, Ellie was still a vibrant storyteller, the go-to person for unraveling the twisted skeins of bloodlines to figure out who was related to whom, the tribal re-memberer of quirks that made long-dead relatives come back to life. The auburn lights had faded in her hair, but her mane was still thick enough to rouse envy in the non–senior citizen population. Her fingernails were as long and glamorous as the ones that had clasped fancy drinks in the heyday of her youth. Her appetite for life and the dramas of family and friends was as voracious as ever. That day she was reduced to recapping all the celebrity scandals from the supermarket tabloids piled up on the nearby shelf under her kitchen television, since her own hell-raising days were behind her. She moved on to family news and then, with the mischievous look of a naughty child setting off a firecracker, she blew up the world as I knew it.

"You know," she said, her eyes on me as she exhaled her dragon smoke, "when your mother married my brother, your uncle Joe looked at her passport and the name on it wasn't her maiden name."

It took a full ten seconds to close my mouth and I only did so after Ellie prompted me.

"You're catchin' flies."

"Wait," I said. "Wait," stalling for time. "Ma married the . . . the hunchback?"

But instead of my mother and the hunchback, I thought of the heart-shaped bronze box, the one I found while snooping through my parents' bureau one day when they were out, the day I discovered the proof I was adopted. I was ten and believed that I had been somehow switched at birth. If my parents weren't officially married, it made a skewed sense that I didn't belong to them either, that they had gotten me from somewhere unofficial, somewhere not approved by the Catholic Church. And wasn't the fact that I was adopted hinted at regularly by my not-mother? Wasn't that her unfailing *cri de coeur*, her amen to every argument: "*You not from this-a family*"? I knew she was right; in fact, I wanted her to be right. If the family didn't want me, then I didn't want them either. I would go and live with one of the black-and-white perfect American families from the television sitcoms I watched every night after supper. I belonged in one of those sunny families where voices were never raised and problems were resolved with a laugh track. I tried to ferret out the truth about my adoption whenever I could. I searched the house for the official papers on the rare occasions I was home alone. I hovered at the edges of family feasts hoping for the dropped crumbs of clues from my adult relatives, even though most times they were speaking Italian, and an incomprehensible dialect version of Italian at that. There were definitely things that didn't add up in my family history, secret adult things that could possibly be hidden information about my real mother.

On Memorial Day I had gone with my father to Calvary Cemetery, a treeless expanse of ornate immigrant gravestones not far from our house. I was thrilled that he took just me and not my princeling little brother and baby sister. Memorial Day was a serious holiday in our Italian American community. Old ladies immured in black dresses and stockings set up lawn chairs for all-day visits with their dead husbands. Graves were decorated lavishly with wreaths and flowers. Sweltering neighbors greeted one another, threading their way through the closely placed stones under the merciless sun. The stones reminded me with a pang of the overcrowded teeth in my own mouth that portended the looming horror of braces. We visited familiar family graves and a new one I didn't know. The name on the tombstone was "Josephine," and she had our surname—Leone. My normally exuberant father, he of the roaring laugh and impromptu operatic aria, was silent and removed as he stood over the grave, head bowed. Afterward, we visited an elderly couple who lived at the very edge of the cemetery, like Hadean gatekeepers who had only to open their back door to grant entrance to the world of the dead. The tiny couple spoke Italian. They were benign looking despite the grisly gatekeeping duties I imagined they performed in the dark of night. The little old lady had a cloud of soft white hair and a kindly manner; her husband was thin and aloof. I knew they weren't relatives, but my father addressed them as "Ma" and "Papá." Secret grandparents I had never met? My only living grandparent was my grandfather, my father's father, who lived with us and spent most of his time in the basement reading *Il Progresso*, the Italian-language newspaper, and smoking his manure-smelling Parodi cigars that must have reminded him of the farm back in San Donato Val di Comino. Was my father using some random Italian honorific with the gatekeepers, the way I called my parents' close friends "Zi," dialect for "Aunt" or "Uncle"? I wandered into the living room, restless, as the adults spoke Italian. I stood in shock, open mouthed, at what I saw in that room. I had the stomach-dropping sensation of someone on a carnival ride. This couple had a big, framed baby picture *of me* on the wall. I was jiggling with curiosity. But some formal sadness in my father's manner with them made me hesitate to ask who they were and why my baby picture was at their strange house in a place of honor.

For the next few weeks after Memorial Day, I bided my time, my Nancy Drew skills straining my leash, my curiosity an ephemeral companion hovering over me like the guardian-angel stalkers the nuns were always babbling about. Finally, the day came. My mother was safely trapped in some tedious task downstairs, my little brother and sister planted in front of the television stupefied by cartoons. I sneaked upstairs and searched my parents' bureau drawers, on the alert for a pause in the sound of the knife snicking against the pasta board downstairs. I found my father's neatly folded boxer shorts, ironed white handkerchiefs, and a leather box of cufflinks. But in the very top drawer, the one I could only reach on my toes, there was an ornate heart-shaped bronze box tucked into the farthest corner. I carefully lifted it out and slid the cover off, mouth-breathing like I had just outrun every barking dog on the block.

The world had tilted that day when I opened the box and released the sad exhalations of lost love. I found the top of a wedding cake with a tiny bride and groom standing under a dented wire arch with yellowed muslin flowers. There was a delicate white-gold ring I tried on my own finger. The ring looked a travesty on my grubby, nail-bitten hand. There was no inscription. Finally, there was a picture of my father with another woman, a beautiful young girl with dark hair who wasn't my mother. Well, now I had proof. Of what, I wasn't sure, but it was proof that my mother and father had secrets, grown-up secrets that meant that the everyday world of our family wasn't what it seemed to be. I slowly realized that this was the proof that I was adopted and my mother wasn't my real mother and this dark-haired slender ghost-woman was my real mother. My heart began to pound and all I heard was my own thumping pulse, racing at the speed of a hopping rabbit under the shadow of a hawk. I hoped it was true. The young woman in the picture looked American. Really American, unlike my fake American mother, who had a US birth certificate somewhere but was in reality a farm girl from the Italian Apennines who couldn't speak English without mangling it. This woman was probably like Aunt Ellie, normal, I thought, staring at the curling photograph. I was sure she went to school in this country and had never flapped her teacher's undies on river rocks to get out of social studies. She looked like she read books, like she had graduated from high school. She looked like she could be my mother. She *was* my mother, and this impersonator who lived with me, who kept trying to lure me into her spidery embrace, was my evil stepmother, not the woman who birthed me. My real mother died tragically young, giving birth to me, and I had been robbed of her. I had the proof in my hands. This was Josephine, the name I had seen on the tombstone. Here was my real mother, whom I nicknamed Jo, like my favorite character in *Little Women*. The elderly couple were my grandparents. That's why they had my baby picture on their wall. I couldn't wait to visit them again and hear about my real mother. I could ride my bike. I pictured myself sitting with my grandmother, eating delicious pastries she had made just for me, and having her tell me I looked just like Jo. This fantasy shattered when I recalled that they hadn't spoken a word of English the entire time my father had been with them on the visit. They had only smiled and nodded at me.

It took only a week to also shatter the stepmother myth. It could've happened sooner, but math was not my strong point. I was still staying after school at least twice a week for not scoring a passing grade in the daily "mental arithmetic" tests. I couldn't add on paper, and juggling numbers in my head was impossible. Even telling time was a challenge. Actually, I couldn't tell time but had been faking it for so long I couldn't admit I had no idea what "quarter to eight" meant. Which is why I was unable to subtract the four digits of Josephine's death date chiseled into her tombstone from my own much later birth date. I dwelled then mainly in the realm of magical thinking. The same nuns who were trying to get me to mentally add and subtract numbers were non-ironically pushing guardian angels and miracles and the deliciously horrible story of how Saint Rita got the thorn permanently suppurating in the middle of her

forehead (it flew at her like a guided missile from Jesus's crown of
thorns one day when she was praying in front of Him on the cross).
These same nuns who were spinning tales of magic and horror inexplicably wanted me to compute how many jellybeans Jimmy had
to divide among his friends. Math just couldn't compete with the
lurid and the fantastical. It was like asking if I would rather watch
Dracula sink his fangs into a tender neck or do my parents' taxes.
At that time I believed the Virgin Mary could at any given moment
shimmer with blue abandon in a corner of my bedroom. I believed
that I could make the rag dolls in the painting above my bed come
to life if I prayed hard enough. I believed angry Indians could gal-
lop down Bridge Street, surround my house, and trap us indoors,
whooping and yipping while I cowered in a closet. I believed Jo
was my mother, as fiery and intelligent as Jo in *Little Women*. I pictured her as tomboyish in a pert, American way, like Doris Day. Or
dressed in her suit in the photograph, cracking wise and leaning
sexily against a desk like Rosalind Russell in *His Girl Friday*.

A week after The Discovery, my imposter mother kissed me
good-bye and I bounded giddily into the backseat of Auntie Ellie
and Uncle Benny's car. I was spending the whole summer with
them in their house by the sea. I would see my real father and fake
mother only on weekends, when they and about thirty other friends
drove down from our Boston suburb in a caravan of Chevys to
spend the day at the beach. Auntie Ellie and Uncle Benny had thirteen acres of land with a bayside beach and a two-hundred-year-old
house shared with Uncle Benny's younger brother, Johnny, and
his wife, Camille.

It was Ellie who had explained the mystery that summer when
I was ten. Josephine was daddy's first wife, who had died of a bad
heart at the age of twenty-three. The drama kept intensifying as
Ellie went on with her story. Josephine was pregnant when she
died in my father's arms. She was laid out in our parlor in her
white wedding dress, right under the porch windows where the
nubbly beige sofa was situated today. I had a morbid, guilty thrill

picturing young, tragic Josephine lying like Snow White in her casket, veiled in white lace, a replica of her wedding bouquet clasped in her folded icy fingers. Josephine's ghost would haunt the living room forevermore and my late-night movie viewing would always be fueled by an extra frisson of fear no matter what the movie was about. I would lie on the sofa and think, "Her head was right here where mine is. She was lying in her coffin, just like I am right now. Only she was dead."

Ellie continued her story, telling me that my father, brokenhearted at Josephine's death, took off on an extended cross-country trip with his buddies. Ellie's mother, my grandmother, cried and prayed until the day he stepped over the threshold of our house. But he returned home with his heart still in tatters and went wild, dating all kinds of women, frightening my grandmother—until Ellie brought my mother home and my father agreed to settle down with a nice young girl from the old country, the official story I had always been told. The Josephine Is My Real Mother fantasy was proof only of my own ability to draw insanely illogical conclusions out of thin air, an excitable nature, and a preteen disposition toward tragedy fueled by the endless supply of Ellie's *True Confessions* magazines kept in the bathroom closet. If you held up a picture of my actual mother and one of me, you would see our twin widow's peaks, our identical noses, our matching sad meatball eyes. My mother was my real mother, Ellie assured me. She opened a kitchen drawer and pulled out the scrap paper she used for grocery lists, then she clarified with a math proficiency honed by countless games of gin rummy the impossibility of Josephine being the American mother of my cherished longings. Even I could see the dates didn't work.

Now I wanted Ellie to unravel another mystery. I reached for one of Ellie's cigarettes and lit up.

"Did she? Marry the hunchback?" I asked. Ellie didn't know. "All I know is, that wasn't her maiden name on the passport. That's what Uncle Joe told me," she said.

"And you can't say anything to your mother either or you'll get Uncle Joe in trouble," she continued, taking another deep drag of her cigarette, inhaling and squinting through the smoke halo framing her like a demented saint. All of the long-dormant questions about the secrets my mother harbored came springing back to life.

"Are you telling me you knew my mother all these years, you two are like sisters, and you never once asked her about this?" I said, my voice time traveling all the way back into a preadolescent squeak of outrage.

Ellie folded her arms, sat back, and looked at me like I was indeed a dopey ten-year-old. She clucked her irritation.

"'Course I asked her." In her thick Boston accent "'course" sounded like "caws." "Your mother got all huffy and yelled at me. She said, 'Your brother and I told each other everything, and if you have any questions, ask him.'"

I knew better than to ask if Ellie ever went to her brother with that question. We were bonded in our reverence for my father. Daddy was thirteen years older than Ellie and more her father than her brother. Even years after his premature death, Ellie couldn't speak of his loss without tears. He was one of those sun kings around whom people orbited, and we were his closest and most devout satellites, constantly craving his warmth and attention, fearing his displeasure. I wouldn't have risked asking him either.

"Don't say nothing to your mother," Ellie said again. "I don't want to listen to her. I'll never hear the end of it." I promised Ellie I wouldn't tell my mother about Uncle Joe finding the passport so many years ago. But I didn't promise her I wouldn't resurrect my long-dormant Nancy Drew detective skills and find out about the passport in question in some other way.

The idea came to me after my mother talked about having a psychic over to read the cards for her and her friends. My mother, who scoffed at the rituals of the Catholic Church (she was an ally when I abandoned it, but not for the same reasons), was a firm believer in all manner of supernatural rituals. She was cynical to the core about human nature and professed no belief in the after-life at all, since my father had only appeared in a dream once to complain about the state of the yard that had been his pride and joy in life and was now becoming derelict, according to his dream self. My mother thought priests were slackers and nuns deluded prisses who preferred marriage to a ghost to a real man, and accepted none of their doctrines or catechisms. However, if a psychic told her a revelation divined from the cards, she automatically suspended all disbelief, like those instant converts thudding to the floor in dead faints on religious revival shows.

Nancy Drew solved mysteries in her polite WASPy way without ever breaking rules; I needed to break all the rules of filial obligation and invoke my homey, Machiavelli, to get to the bottom of my mother's possible marriage to the hunchback.

I did it over coffee one morning when she was spending the weekend with us. My mother was now in her late seventies, still feisty and mordantly funny.

"Hey, Ma, guess what? I went to a psychic, and she said something about you!"

"Oh, yeah?" My mother leaned in, hooked. "She tell you I'm gonna die?"

My mother made jokes about dying all the time to stick it to death and show it she was not afraid.

"No, she said something weird I didn't understand. Something about you being, uh, in love with or engaged or something to someone in the old country?"

There were no wiseass comebacks. Instead, the color drained from my mother's face so dramatically I felt alarmed and a little guilty. Now looking like Dracula's host, she stammered a garbled reply and looked away. I changed the subject, worried I had gone too far.

But just a few weeks later, my mother made a dramatic pronouncement at my kitchen table.

"Ho-kay, I tell you my story," she blurted, as if I had just tased her. Figuratively, I guess I had been poking her, hoping the truth would tumble out at last. I wondered at this moment whether I wanted to hear it.

"My mother sold me."

My mother, with possible genetic ties to storied actress Eleanora Duse guiding her delivery, paused and checked to see that my jaw was effectively unhinged. (It was.) And then she told me her story.

The real one, at last, not the official account.

It was a version I should've been able to figure out for myself. My mother said more than once that she was born in this country, even though she still struggled with the language and had no memory of her time here as a baby. It was logical that she should use her American passport to barter her way back to this country. How else would she be able to go against her father's iron decree and get to America? Her mother didn't have any money of her own. But my mother, born here, had an American passport, a golden ticket out of an enslaved marriage and a narrow escape from the coming Nazi occupation of her hometown. Where did she get the money? That had to come from the man her mother found who wanted to immigrate to America. The complete stranger my mother married in Naples before boarding the ship.

My skinny eighteen-year-old mother married a total stranger and shared a cabin with him for the two weeks it took to cross the ocean to an unknown destination, where she was met by a stern aunt she barely remembered, and then divorced this same stranger just a month later, never to see him again. I pictured the close quarters of the cabin, how jumpy and watchful I would be in her situation, and I thought of the sparrow that flew into my kitchen from the open slider, how the frenzy for escape emanating from its tiny body took up the entire room. "Weren't you afraid?" I asked my mother. "What if he raped you? He could say you were married, after all," I said. "What if he thought it was his 'right'?"

"No," my mother assured me. "He was a gentleman," she said firmly, looking me in the eye.

My sardonic mother, whose wounded eyes put the lie to all her tough talk, felt shame all of her life for being put between the rock of her intractable father and the hard place the church assigned her after she balked at a forced marriage and blew town. Along with defiance and relief at her narrow escape, she felt *vergonia*, the burning, irrational humiliation that poor people feel about their hard lives and hard choices. This auto-da-fé, the ceremony of judgment when her mother-in-law's friends talked about her, when the priests barred her from the rites of a sanctioned marriage, was the price she paid for her new life.

And what could she do when her daughter and chief inquisitor asked her to prove the validity of her current marriage, the real one, again and again by the silly measure of a white dress?

My mother did what she could. She told me a fairy tale, the official story, the version all immigrants tell when they reinvent themselves, and hoped for the best.

Mother, Mother, Mother

"I could be fierce about a child; I know it."

That was me, being prescient in my twenties. In the usually overwrought and self-pitying pages of my journal at that time, I was trying to imagine what it would be like to mother a child, a galactic leap for my immature self.

"This is theoretical. It would have to be a different life, a different time; I would have to conquer in myself that reserve I have to giving myself over to the possession, the *inevitability* of it all. The ordinariness."

That was me, not being prescient. Our son, Jesse, was the farthest thing away from ordinary, from his extremely premature birth to his untimely death at the age of seventeen.

I saw Jesse moments after he was born and before he was whisked away, and I had no hesitation giving myself over to the possession, the inevitability of it all. The fierce love I had predicted in my twenties was there, as if it had always been there, waiting to be born along with him in the dramatic first moments of his arrival ten weeks early. After an effortless, healthy pregnancy, one day in October my immune system broke down and I ran a high temperature and contracted what I thought was the flu. Our baby wasn't due until New Year's Day. After an evening of vomiting and pain, my midwife told me I was in labor when I called and to come to the hospital as soon as we could. My husband, Chris, and I had trouble getting a cab outside our apartment in Hell's Kitchen, which wasn't surprising in the least. We looked like the climactic scene from a disaster movie as Chris flung open the door in a feral panic and I remained on my hands and knees being sick on the sidewalk. The driver protested, but my husband refused to listen and shepherded me into the cab. Once in the taxi, with every pothole from 48th Street to Saint Vincent's Hospital in the Village cruelly punctuating the labor pains that had begun, I croaked to my husband between gasps, "It's too soon. The baby probably won't make it." The rest of Jesse's birth day is a blur, with faces floating to the surface then fading away from a limbo state of pain and anxiety: the jolly Irish nurse wearing the "Are we having fun yet?" button; Chris, helplessness and fear softening his features; another nurse giving me a standup routine on childbirth cries according to ethnicity. Finally, Jesse's arrival later that day, his emergence into the world without drugs, three pounds, seven ounces, with high Apgar scores, breathing on his own, his cry a reassurance of his presence in this world.

It would be almost two months before I held him in my arms.

My mother's reaction to the news of Jesse's early birth was so frenzied that it had the opposite effect of calming me down, her worry washing over me like a warm bath. "It's too soon!" she kept shrieking into the phone, eerily echoing what I had said in the cab, her normally low voice in a register used specifically for the coffin-side cries at wakes. I reassured her, and myself, that he was alive and well, our tiny man-child in his plastic box, skin mottled

and purple, strained features showing little hint of the almost sur-
real, lit-from-within beauty that would flower in the months ahead.
The nurses insisted I sit in a wheelchair and I was dismissive,
until I saw him. The first sight of our child made me gasp. My legs
were suddenly weak. He breathed through a tube and there were
lines invading his filament veins delivering mysterious and unset-
tling liquids to his tiny body. A jiggling readout displayed numbers
measuring oxygen and other vital signs. Despite all of this, Jesse's
medical team was hopeful: his weight was good, better than most
thirty-week preemies, and he appeared to thrive according to the
incomprehensible bleeping numbers.

All of that changed on the third day of Jesse's life, when he
suffered a grade-four intraventricular hemorrhage and coded blue
in our presence. Now the prognosis turned grim, and my mother's
anxious calls were nagging echoes of my own fears, sapping the
strength I needed to sit by Jesse's incubator and will him to life,
the only thing I could do besides pump breast milk and stare at
the incomprehensible numbers on the machines that were both
tyrannizing and saving my son.

Finally, almost two months after his birth, we brought Jesse
home. Free of the shrill machines, the over-bright lights, the sanitized atmosphere of dread, we couldn't stop nestling, snuggling,
cradling, celebrating our baby. I wore him in a sling all day, close
to my heart. Ma disapproved. In one of her worry-wrought calls
she fretted, "You ken' hold 'im all day." But I did. I held him all
day and he slept with us at night, his pretty bassinet with the tiny
yellow rosebuds sitting idly by. I needed to reclaim him from the
sanitized stink of the hospital, the overbearing doctors, the caring
nurses, the social workers whose questions felt like intrusions. It
didn't occur to me that some of Ma's worry might be for my own
stamina and health. Her disapproval seemed like a decree from
yet one more official person telling me how to mother my child. I
resented her. I thought she was jealous of my love being directed
away from her and to my child.

"Ma is afraid of Jesse" —Journal, October 10, 1988

But in the snapshot I have of Ma with Jesse on that first trip home to Boston with him, she is holding him across her lap and smiling as he looks up at her. She shows no fear, just love and confidence as she handles him as she would any of her other grandchildren. It is only now that I see my defensiveness mirrored back at me, falsifying what was before my own eyes. I was the one who was afraid—afraid my mother would regard my child as damaged and recoil from him.

When Jesse was a little older, in the first of our mother-daughter role reversals, I showed Ma how to feed Jess, depressing the spoon on his tongue to avoid thrusting; how to seat him facing outwards, her knee between his legs to prevent spastic scissoring. It felt strangely familiar to me, this reverse mothering, until I realized that this is the feeling that comes from being the child of an immigrant. I had traversed this road before, explaining the way something worked to my mother. I had been her (unwilling) interpreter when an official-sounding person called and their cultivated tones made my mother react in terror and forget how to speak English. I had, with irritation, explained the plotlines to movies that had British actors, that specific accent immediately turning what they said to gibberish in Ma's brain. I had signed my own report cards, my mother's signature too hesitant and garbled, and her disinterest in my grades only too apparent.

Now that I was a mother, I thought often about how Ma had been mothered. I knew she had lost her mother when she was still a teenager and had immigrated to this country. As with anything about her own childhood, Ma had not been forthcoming except for the occasional mystifying remark. She told me once that her mother slept with her, in her bed. Was that every night? What did that say about her mother's marriage, which I knew to be troubled to the point of frequent violent scenes? Did her mother's unhappiness spill over to the way she interacted with her only child? Was Ma an afterthought? A burden? My mother had said, starkly, that her mother didn't love her father and was planning to leave him for someone else during the brief time they lived in the United States. Did that mean my grandmother was planning to abandon my mother, then only an infant, for this new man she loved? I asked my mother this question, and she shrugged. I was so taken aback I didn't ask further.

At any rate, the mother figure my grandmother entrusted with Ma was her older sister, the one I knew as the formidable Great-Aunt Mary. "Scary Mary," as I had privately named her, had put my mother to work mere days after her arrival in this country. Mary herself had been a mail-order bride, and Ma had recounted in hushed tones the story of how her aunt's husband had falsely sent another, handsomer man's photograph and that after he had done her the vast benevolence of marrying her at Ellis Island, he had raped my great-aunt on the first night of their marriage like a beast taking his prey. But by the time I knew Great-Aunt Mary, the beast was just a cowering drunk, and even as a child I understood that she was the one with the power. She was a fairy-tale queen to us as children exploring her enchanted realm, an apple orchard and trout farm out in the country with an actual in-ground swimming pool, the first private one I had ever seen. Great-Aunt Mary was gruff with children and that may have been because she spoke very little English. She had white hair and a shelf-like bosom and piercing blue eyes. Ma hinted that she was a *strega* and told me she had once healed my little brother when he was sick as a baby, spending the entire night alone with him, refusing entry to anyone else and doing mysterious shamanic things Ma couldn't describe. I was both fascinated and frightened. I didn't want Scary Mary alone with me in my room at night.

Despite her compromised English and her useless sot of a husband, Great-Aunt Mary had been an astute businesswoman, creating a one of a kind business, selling dresses to factory workers in Lowell from a bus she drove herself, then establishing stores in Boston's suburbs before investing in the apple orchard and trout farm. She eventually bought a motel in Fort Lauderdale and sent my mother a picture of herself in a bathing suit she had crocheted herself. Standing beside her was a man half her age in a Speedo and dark glasses, looking like an Italian gigolo from Central Casting. I couldn't help but admire Great-Aunt Mary's divine excess, but I also couldn't forget that she had banished my mother shortly after she arrived in this country because of the jealousy of her adopted son. When I think of my mother's loneliness and terror at the age of eighteen, sent to live with strangers because of her aunt's callousness or cowardice or both, my admiration for Great-Aunt Mary withers away. What is left is awe for my mother's long, lonely journey of self-mothering until she had her own family. Awe and guilt, my evil twins, live side by side in my thoughts, the guilt for all the times I pushed her away.

Motherhood did not come easily to anyone in my family. My aunt Ellie lost three babies. My aunt Sara never had children. My mother was an only child. And my mother took years to conceive me. Specialists in Boston told her there was no hope. Ma confided to me once that she watched my father sitting alone and worried that he was thinking of his first wife, the one that died young, pregnant with his child that never was. She wondered if he felt cursed. She agonized that she might never have a child. Finally, without the help of the specialists, but with some antique version of hormone shots given by the local Italian American general practitioner, Dr. Amendola, she was able to conceive me.

In Ma's place, I would have been giddy, unable to believe my luck at the avalanche of blessings, the lonely only child who had been gifted an entire new family that knew how to laugh, that enjoyed company, and feasting and parties and dressing up at *carnivale*, and to live comfortably, in peace, amid plenty, all this while married to a man who was passionate, not violent like her father, this man who loved her without limit. And my mother was joyful,

as I remember her, for the fifteen years she had left of this kind
of happiness, before my father died. But there was always a wari-
ness there, too, as if she sensed it could all be snatched away by a
random and cruel *destino* decreed by some barbaric and capricious
god. Unbridled joy attracts the jealousy of others; their envy brings
down a curse upon you if you are foolish enough to remain unpro-
tected or show your bliss to the world. This Ma had been taught
and this she believed more dogmatically and with more fervor than
any tenet of the church. And she was right to be wary because after
my father was snatched from her, ending her world, she still had to
be a mother to us all: my twelve-year-old brother, my seven-year-old
sister, and my sullen, contorted, rageful fifteen-year-old self, her
greatest maternal challenge.

———————

Is how we mother defined by how we were mothered? I read an
article in *Scientific American* that said the cells of a baby always
remain within the mother even after the baby physically leaves the
mother's womb. Is that what it means, to yearn forevermore for
the flesh that is within you but without you? When Ma's mother
died of peritonitis six months after Ma left for the United States,
was it her appendix that burst or her heart, cleft with regret because she knew she would never see her daughter again? When I
found Jesse dead on a January morning and my body grew a can-
cerous not-Jesse tumor that weighed what he did at birth, was that
the physical embodying of my terrible yearning for him, twisted
and poisoned by grief? We have our mother's cells in our bodies,
and our children's cells, too. It's called *microchimerism*, this cell
thing. After the chimera in Greek mythology: a fire-breathing female monster with a lion's head, a goat's body, and a serpent's tail.
"I could be fierce about a child," I wrote in my clueless twenties.
Then I had a child and had to fight for his right to be regarded
as fully human despite his disabilities. I became a fire-breathing

female monster because I was re-birthed in the place being a mother can take you, the place you can never, ever imagine before you go there, but when you are there, it is as familiar as the walls of the womb where you once lived.

My mother and father pose in our yard for a jokey picture. They haven't been married long. My mother faces the camera, smiling widely. She is wearing a light-colored dress with puffy sleeves. She is thick in the middle. My dad faces her, looking down at a discreet bulge beneath her dress. He is smiling, too, and at the same time affects a perplexed look, his hand on his chin, mugging for the un-seen audience. My mother and father are obviously celebrating the bulge, telling the world, spreading their joy, using the photograph as a cute birth announcement.

But there is no baby. My mother is having a hysterical preg-nancy, one that lasts for six months, she later tells me. I don't know whether to believe her. I thought only animals had hyster-ical pregnancies. My awe of Ma increases at the thought of the mind power involved in fooling her own reproductive system to stop menstruation and produce a phantom bulge. What kind of longing is that? How do you trick your own body into mimicking gestation? And is that what I inherited from her when I created the reverse, the not-Jesse tumor that arose out of my own ceaseless longing for him after he was irretrievably gone from my life? An ability that can mold your body, make it the slave of your hopeless yearning? After my son died I began to die, too, which was my only remaining desire in the grayed-out limbo world of grief I inhab-ited. I longed for oblivion, an end to the visceral pain of losing my son. My body mocked my pregnancy and grew an ugly tumor that was the same size as my son at birth. The not-Jesse, a three-pound mutant horror of blood and ganglia, was excised and removed. My mother's trick womb deflated after she was told there was no baby.

Maybe it was not a superpower but a disorder passed on like a defective gene. My mother, longing for the phantom child not yet conceived; I, wanting only my son back. She created air, a bubble of hope for what could be, and I fashioned a monster ball of flesh, born of despair for losing what was.

My little brother, the princeling of the Leone family, a cherub-faced blond toddler and the answer to my mother's fervent prayers, was the person I most wanted gone from my life. I was five years old, three years older than Michael. Before his arrival I had been the storied, long-awaited first child. I lived in a house that had not only my adoring parents but also a glut of live-in relatives, every one of them rapturous and ready to dote on the new baby. But the golden era of me only lasted three years. I had been usurped by my brother's arrival, my crown snatched, my princess reign curtailed. I no longer basked in the beam of my father's sun. My mother, too, had receded, bedazzled, drunk on my brother's beauty, his curls, his happy baby chortles.

Michael and I were alone in the parlor, the adult voices far away. I felt safe and cushioned by the laughter of the grown-ups and familiar smells of pastry and anisette coming from the kitchen. The coffee table in the parlor had a cut-glass bowl of salted peanuts on it. The coffee table was magic because it came up to my waist, just like the kitchen table Ma used when she stood before it like a wizard, making delicious things out of mounds of flour and eggs. I took two peanuts out of the bowl. I was as careful and precise as my mother ladling out *minestra*. I put one peanut in front of Michael and the other one on my side of the table. I spoke in Ma's voice. I said, "You hungry, *mammá?*" in the syrupy voice my mother used to talk to my baby brother. My mother referred to all of her children as herself. I grew up hearing her address me as herself, as in "You want some macaroni, *mammá?*" or "Finish your tonic, *mammá.*" This was a feature, I realized many years later, of the way many southern Italians speak in dialect to their children. On the episode of *The Sopranos* when Tony goes to Naples, I heard the familiar sound of Italian spoken in a southern dialect so juicy it was like eating dribbly ripe figs in the warm caress of a Mediterranean sun. During this attack of television-induced synesthesia, I levitated through time and space and no longer inhabited my adult body, floating serenely in the cloud-unconscious of childhood memories. The exact Proustian moment came when the female Mafia boss/goddess in human form introduced her prepubescent son to Tony as herself. "Bella mammá," she says, cradling her son's chin as she gazes at him with love. Literal translation: "Beautiful mother." Other translation: *This is my son who is not fully himself because he is a part of me.*

When I was five, I thought that my mother called Michael by her own name because he was still part of her, like a vital organ, but I wasn't, not anymore. I was a loose tooth, rotten and wobbly and about to fall out.

In the living room, I tossed a peanut in the air and opened my mouth, catching it. "You do it," I commanded. Michael's chubby hands imitated mine and he threw the peanut in a clumsy arc. He caught the peanut in his mouth, gleeful, happy to please me, his pretend *mammá*. He chuckled his adorable baby laugh, the one that made my mother swoon. He choked. He turned blue.

There was a roiling and a tempest as the adult voices converged and became a shrieking gale, and the speeded up actions of the adults blurred the world, covering my brother, who was taken up into the eye of the storm. Then there was quiet, and I became invisible.

A month later, crouched in a front row seat on the staircase in our hallway, I stared through the banisters at my weeping mother. "He called the nurse '*mammá*,'" she wailed. My father looked helpless and dangerous because he was helpless. My aunt offered coffee and her own quick tears. No one saw me. I shuddered at the enormity of my five-year-old power. I had wished my brother gone and now he was.

"They moved him to Children's," my mother told my aunt, who must have been watching me while they were at the hospital. I didn't know what "Children's" meant and no one explained it to me. Before, they told me he was in the hospital. I knew what the hospital was, the place of my parents' worst betrayal only the year before. They had delivered me under false pretenses to a scarily cheery nurse at the hospital. I was to have my tonsils out, my parents leaving me there after luring me with ice cream and a story about touring the hospital. (Not the last time in my life I was credulous with painful results.) They were both complicit in the lies that abandoned me at the hospital, but I blamed Ma and not my father for the double cross. I knew that the hospital was a bad place, where people dressed like ghosts put rubber masks over your terrified face. But "Children's" sounded even more ominous. I thought it might be like the deceptively titled Pleasure Island in the Pinocchio movie where bad boys went and were turned into donkeys. I wanted to tell the people that were keeping Michael in Children's that he was a good boy, and that I, his sister, knew he was good, that he didn't deserve to be sent away. But I was invisible, and the wishing away of my brother had gone wrong, like a fairy tale with a bad ending. My brother had disappeared but I had not been restored to my former glory; instead I had vanished, too, and my mother and my father couldn't find me even though I was right there on the stairs, looking at them through the polished oak bars.

What was it like for my mother in that long month when her son was hospitalized? I know what it was like. I am sure that the world collapsed like a dying star and turned everything around her into a black hole. It did for me. I am sure that time elongated into the hopeless limbo of unbaptized souls, the ones I learned about in catechism, who lived in a place where waiting went on and on without end, for eternity, spiked by moments of fear and pain and the inability to ever, ever see God. It did for me. I am sure that it felt like everyone else in this new limbo world existed as gatekeepers to prevent my mother from seeing my brother. That's how I felt, too, when my son, Jesse, was in the neonatal intensive care unit for the first two and a half months of his life.

My mother's reaction when she first saw my son in the high-tech hospital world that was his first home puzzled me at first. The over-lit, sterile room where Jesse lay smelled of nothing but electronics and the acrid fear of bereft parents. The beeping plastic shields that acted as barriers between parents and their fragile infants assaulted my mother. She acted like someone transported to an alien space station. She backed away. She acted nervous; she was stiff-bodied. While my aunt and sister caressed Jesse and murmured his name, claiming him for our tribe, my mother could barely look at him. She hovered behind my aunt and my sister, made the sign of the cross in the air in Jesse's general direction, and moved away. I was disappointed at what I saw as her inability to overcome her fear to welcome my son into the world. I was contemptuous of her cringing response. I felt that I understood her gut-level reaction, because I saw how terrifying this laboratory filled with silent, wizened infants could look. It was terrifying to me, too. But she didn't deserve to be fearful, I thought. It was *my* child that was in this place, not hers.

And it never occurred to me, even once, that she could be remembering her own experience with my brother. The long days and even longer nights. The lack of information from the medical staff and the condescension of the doctors. The inability to get to

Boston except by a long trolley ride for someone who couldn't drive a car. Forbidden to hold, touch, smell her baby hidden away behind the white iron crib, the plastic sheeting in a setting eerily similar to the neonatal intensive care unit.

Why does it take so long to learn compassion? Why does a meteor-sized hole need to crash through your own heart before you can understand someone else's sorrow? Or it could be that my use of the plural "you" is wrong. Maybe it's my own character flaw, or the limits of my pre-Jesse judgmental, undersized heart. After Jesse, my heart expanded and became normal. Or, as my mother once put it, sitting at my kitchen table: "You were a bitch. Not now. But then." I agreed with her. I held my own son. And I addressed him as "*mammá*" without even thinking, kissing him, making him giggle, feeding him, in all the love-struck delirium and lost boundaries of motherhood.

02458
The Lake

Newton, Massachusetts, is an upscale leafy suburb about seven miles from downtown Boston. It has graceful Tudor houses with huge, manicured backyards. The city hosts the sprawling red-brick campus of Boston College in the six-figure income zone known as Chestnut Hill. In Newton Centre there are boutiques selling one-of-a-kind dresses and restaurants offering pricey cocktails and artisanal dishes. When I tell people I grew up in Newton, they're impressed. They assume my family had big bucks. "Wrong side of the tracks," I tell them: my home was in the Lake, my house across the street from the Raytheon factory where every afternoon at four, hundreds of people spilled out onto the sidewalk bordering our yard, weary and glazed from a day of making widgets.

The official name for the Lake is Nonantum, but no one who lives there calls it that. "I'm goin' up the Lake," you would yell breezily as you ran out the door. There's no lake in the Lake; what was once Silver Lake dried up. By the early sixties it was a green-slicked, toxic puddle behind the Ucinite factory on Nevada Street, where my mother and aunt Ellie worked during World War II and

I later worked for two whole weeks, as long as I could stand repeating the same motion to make mystifying plastic devices for eight hours a day on an assembly line. When I was a kid, we ice-skated on what little of the lake was left, back when we still had winters.

The Madonna del Carmine is paraded down Adams Street every year in July, festooned with dollar bills, a procession that was viewed with distaste by the Irish American nuns who taught me. The same feast is held in San Donato Val di Comino, the mountain village in central Italy that is the *gemello*, or twin city to Nonantum and the ancestral home of most of the Lake's inhabitants. My father's bar, Leone's Café, was on that same street, once called "Bottle Alley," because of the drinking habits of its denizens, I presume. Adams Street ends at Our Lady Help of Christians church, rectory, and schools. There was once a convent there, too, that housed my tormentors for thirteen years, the Sisters of Saint Joseph and members of the cult of Holy Self Abnegation, to which I adhered, briefly. Along Adams Street and next door to Leone's Café was Magni's Bakery, which produced the giant round, hard-crusted loaves we ate in our house, and across the street and down a block was Larry's Superette that provided the logs of provolone Ma lugged down the South Shore every month to rescue my aunt Ellie, who was stranded in Wonder Bread land. The provolone was considered a necessary act of grace, since the only cheese available on the shelves of the local A & P were inedible squares of American, indistinguishable in taste from their plastic wrappers. The Sons of Italy was on Adams Street, along with various other Italian social clubs and our after-school teen hangout in the sixties, Mr. Pup's, the size of a supply closet, and the site of adolescent romances and the inevitable tragedies that followed.

Along Watertown Street, the main thoroughfare that bisected our own, Bridge Street, was the place to buy sausages, DePasquale's, still serving its regulars today and thrilling the foodies who have recently discovered its heavenly garlic-infused links. Further down on the same block was Suzy's, the salon where Ma went once a week to have her hair teased and glued in place. Antoine's Pastry, source of divine cannoli and pine nut–topped cookies, was one block down from Suzy's. Magni's Funeral Home relocated to Watertown Street from Adams Street, across from La Sposa, the place to get your wedding dress, the proximity of the two businesses forcing one to ponder life's beginnings and endings. The tiny park at the end of our street is where the giant Santa Claus was erected every Christmas, his hand raised in a salute to the people who live in the Lake. Columbus Hall, across the street from the park, was the community center where Aunt Ellie was married and where the annual Christmas party was held, with grouchy Santas shuffling through huge plastic bags, aware they could be taking bets on a game down at the club instead of handing out toys to the rowdy children of the Lake.

This was Ma's world for most of her life. Since she only visited Our Lady Help of Christians church for weddings or funerals, her actual temple of worship and community was Dunkin' Donuts, where she could meet cronies, exchange gossip, and place her bets for the day, an offering to the gods of chance, Ma's own version of magical thinking, which mirrored the silent petitions of the old lady believers in church, telling their beads and asking the Madonna for mercy.

Down the street from Dunkin's, along Watertown Street was Hawthorne Park, the preferred location of teenage summer trysts and the site for the carnival during the yearly *festa* that preceded Our Lady of Carmine's wobbly procession down Adams Street. One of the headliners at the carnival was usually an Elvis impersonator, son of the local wise guy and unofficial mayor of the Lake, Fat Pellegrini. Fat was responsible for the crime-free nature of the Lake, along with the neighborhood watch of keen-eyed old ladies in black scanning the horizon from porches and stoops. It was a toss-up as to who was more dangerous to potential evildoers. Hawthorne Park has been renamed Pellegrini Park Recreation

Center after Joanie, the wife of our unofficial mayor, who always nodded to my husband, Chris, and addressed him as "sheriff" out of the side of his mouth, a tribute to the hard-guy film roles my husband had played. Fat was good to the widows and orphans of the Lake, taking up collections and delivering food baskets to the bereaved. The *Boston Globe* once featured him in an article titled with a quote from Fat: "Don't Make a Hero Outta Me—It Stinks." Fat wasn't fat—he was a slender man always; it was just the way of nicknames in the Lake. Chubby wasn't chubby either, and I'm sure Scabby wasn't covered with scabs.

The Lake was famous for having its own language. "Lake talk" was reportedly derived from the carny folk who had come through in the 1930s and '40s. A "mush" (rhymes with "push") was a regular guy and a "divya" was a jerk. A "quister jival" was a pretty girl and to "jol" something was to steal it. Those are the only words I remember hearing as a kid, though there's a whole lexicon available online. It makes sense that our insular world had its own discrete language. The Lake was a singular place, with all the joys and restrictions of a small town, just seven miles from Boston. My friend Susan put it best: "Only in my grandmother's house up the Lake on the poor side of Newton could a bookie, a priest, a police officer, and a bank robber eat at the same table and love each other."

But I bolted from the Lake when I turned eighteen, more aware of its limitations than joys. I wanted a city, not a village. I craved the exotic and scorned what was familiar. I dreamed of escape, living in a place where no one knew my name or could recognize my family bloodline from the shape of my face. The portal to my eventual freedom began with daily visits to a small branch of the Newton Library at the end of my street, of no importance to my mother whatsoever but a trance-inducing holy site for me from the age of five until I became a teenager and found my temporary earthly paradise, the used bookstores of Harvard Square. In the bookstores I discovered the beat poets and heard my first protest songs. The wider world beckoned, first Boston, then New York City.

Every summer in July, the streets of the Lake are painted down the middle with the colors of the Italian flag for the *festa* honoring the Madonna del Carmine. Ma found her village here, her adopted home a world away but still hauntingly familiar, like a lost twin or a recurring dream where the long road you travel brings you to a place you've always known. The Lake is the starting point for me. I'm still skipping along that path, following the red, white, and green road, looking for pieces of myself, realizing there's no place like home for mining the memories you need to build a character or write a story. I'm glad I grew up in the Lake, glad I ran away, and happy to be welcomed back by the cop, the bookie, the priest, and the robber, who most likely all knew my mother and all have a story about her.

Ma Speaks Up

I wish some of the cachet that Italy has now had been around when I was growing up in the late fifties–early sixties. Now the word "Italian" evokes sublime food, sophisticated design, and elegant, sexy lifestyles. We who grew up back then were just "guineas" and "dagos" and "wops," the sons and daughters or grandchildren of impoverished immigrants who narrowly escaped the *miseria* endemic in the backwater south of Italy, the *mezzogiorno*. Southern Italians were parodied endlessly on television, in the movies, and even by our own teachers. (My chubby little brother was Tony Spumoni the Ice Cream Man in his second-grade play.) Our parents talked too loudly and ate foreign food that wasn't appreciated then by foodies; it stank of garlic and left embarrassing oily stains on our lunch bags, shameful reminders of why we were greaseballs and could never be real Americans.

My mother spoke a harsh, guttural dialect from her mountain village in Abruzzi. No mellifluous vowels for her, not the beautiful, standard Tuscan Italian complete with the trilled *r*'s and soft vowels of the *politezza*. Ma spat out the chopped-off ends of words like

the metronomic tocking of a knife on a cutting board. It was ugly
to me then, the sound of my mother's voice. My ear was trained to
hear the melodic trill of American television mothers calling their
children to come in and eat their Jello-mold salads and overcooked
beef. They spoke to them cheerfully, their fluty tones happy and
light. My mother grunted staccato commands and made my name
sound like mud. "Muddy-Ahn."

When I was a kid I was humiliated by my mother's cringing
fear of outsiders, by the way English words would fail her when
speaking on the phone to officials of any kind. Frustrated after only
a few words, she would thrust the phone at me, hissing a command, but I always squirmed away. In my room I could escape to
the closet that housed all my books, a place of magic created by my
father for me when I was four. There I could drown out the sounds
of the garbled curses that followed me up the stairs like a swarm
of angry bees. The outside world, filled with Americans, judged
my mother. I hated the snotty saleswomen who spoke loudly to Ma
when we went to Grover Cronin's for my Easter clothes. My mother
never seemed to notice how they treated her, but I saw how they
thought she was stupid because of her accent, how they smirked at
the way she pronounced words, spoke louder as if she were deaf or
a very small, not-too-bright child. My mother always dressed well;
she had an eye for smart clothes and a delight in them, most likely
nourished by the dearth of available choices in her desolate farm
community. But when my well-dressed mother opened her mouth
it was as if she were wearing rags and a kerchief and standing on
line at Ellis Island begging entry to the New World.

The real reason I hated those salesladies that I couldn't admit
to myself? I agreed with them. I judged her, too. Why couldn't my
mother just hear the right way to talk? How many years had she
been in this country? She really must be stupid. I began to treat her
that way, dismissing her, pushing her away until I no longer felt
ashamed. I felt superior. *I* knew how to talk the right way. In only

a few years, as a preteen mean girl, I would be openly mocking her English, laughing out loud at her sputtering threats that my father would give me an "election" when he got home.

I lived in fear of my mother talking to my teachers, the pillar-of-rectitude nuns who taught me at Our Lady Help of Christians. Long before there was the term "Stockholm syndrome," I had capture-bonded with the sisters of Saint Joseph. I took on their prejudices and lace-curtain Irish airs and self-righteous piety. I knew they would sneer at Ma's imperfect English and her superstitions, and that she would grovel before them like she did sometimes with official people, flattering them like some lickspittle serf appeasing a medieval overlord. The minute they turned their backs would come the bitter, caustic comments. If they knew what she called them! I burned, thinking of my teachers hearing themselves referred to as the "fockin'-a nuns." I pictured two of them, a nun arch. They would lean their veiled heads together and cut their eyes at me, tsking, and regard me forevermore as feral, a child reared by beasts. I would never crown the statue of the Virgin Mary at the May procession.

But I was armed with words, millions of English words retrieved from the books, comics, cereal boxes, Baltimore catechisms, *True Confessions* magazines, Saint Joseph's Daily Missals, Rimbaud poems, and my personal sacred text, Roget's *Thesaurus*. I collected words with the obsessive lust of a true hoarder. I stored my arsenal of word weapons in my brain and kept them at the ready, the long compound nouns, arcane verbs, retro adjectives; the more syllables the better. I wasn't my mother, struck dumb by her own ignorance. At the same time, I knew it was a sin to dishonor your parents by word or deed. I confessed every Saturday to the priest, and my standard go-to sin was "I talked back to my mother." It wasn't a mortal sin, the kind that sent you straight to hell. It was only a venial, the kind you paid for in purgatory later, after you died. I was perfectly content with the "talk back now, pay later" spiritual plan, so even my nun-identified rectitude wasn't challenged by mouthing off to my mother. I sharpened my word skills on her like a knife on a whetstone.

Some of my favorite words in my mean-girl phase:

Cataleptic ("You're just cataleptic—that's how little you know!")

Insipid ("Don't think I'm wearing that insipid pink mohair sweater. Who am I, Annette Funicello?")

Unequivocal ("Allen Ginsburg is an unequivocal genius, but you wouldn't know because you don't read anything, not even a newspaper, much less Beat poetry.")

Voracious ("This family is voracious, and you're a drudge doomed to feed them for the rest of their lives. I'm not hungry.")

Pseudo—spelled and pronounced "swaydo"—("All my swaydo friends are swaydo intellectuals. That's why I have no friends.")

Ma had only one weapon in her quiver. It was silence. My mother's aggrieved, collapsed-star silence held untold reserves of galaxies in its dark and limitless heart. This deep-space silence could go on for days, pinging bursts of pain back and forth between us like gamma rays, leftover energy from the Big Bang argument that started it all in the first place.

When my father died at fifty, my mother's silence was different. She was mute then with sheer terror. This wordless stage came after the fainting, screaming, and trying to pull my father from his coffin by my mother and my extended family. All the Old World drama made me mute with terror, too. My mother and I sat beside each other at Magni's Funeral Home and stared at my father in the coffin. His mouth had a grim set we had never seen in life. Alive, my father had a big smile and a booming laugh, as befitted the owner of a local bar, a man with many friends. Now his waxy hands were clasped around rosary beads—a sanctimonious lie. Like Tutankhamun, he had gold in his coffin, too, a chalice that looked as incongruous there as a golf club, which would have been more meaningful to the life he had lived. I sat erect, my mother in a slump. I hated everyone around me. Like a teenaged Margaret Mead, I watched from a cold-blooded distance and took note of my family wailing and shrieking. I thought of them as primitives unrelated to me. I concentrated on my disdain to keep from joining them; if I did, my screams would dwarf theirs. My father was my idol. He read lots of books, was self-educated, listened to opera, greeted life with joy every day. He didn't have an accent, even though he was born in Italy. He wanted me to go to college. My mother wanted me to get married. He was my ballast and he was gone forever.

The nuns approached the line of mourners. I saw them before my mother did and silently telegraphed a warning to her: sit up straight, act with grace, be polite to my teachers. She didn't get the message. Eyes at half-mast, Ma barely grunted when the first nun took her hand. My mother looked down at her fingers entwined in the nun's, puzzled, as if her hand was dismembered. She seemed mentally deficient. The nun smiled at her. For the first time ever I was seeing the movie version of a sweet-tempered nun in real life, a creature I had believed before this moment to be as fantastical as Tinkerbell.

"God needed him in heaven," the nun murmured. My mother's eyes flew open. Now she seemed galvanized. She sat up straight.

"Fuck God. I need him here," she said, in perfect, non-accented English.

She even pronounced the "h" in the word "him." She was possessed, I later learned, by her future, widowed self.

I wish I could remember what happened immediately after she uttered those words. I wish I could recall the look on the nun's face, or if my Aunt Ellie, sitting on Ma's other side, heard her say "fuck" and giggled aloud, or my own reaction. I can't remember because my brain shut down as if I had lost consciousness and crashed to the floor of Magni's Funeral Home. I can only picture myself, po-faced, stiff-backed, knobby knees together, my thoughts in a galaxy far, far away as I willed myself invisible.

After Ma told God to fuck off, there was no holding her back. Where before her saltiest saying was a mild "sominabitch," with the rest of her curses lost in the tendrils of her unfathomable dialect, now she unleashed her "fucks," "assaholes," and "pricks" upon the unsuspecting world. She possessed the fury of a woman betrayed, first by my father, who introduced her to passion and joy and left her too soon, and then by her own naïve belief that she could be happy forever when she knew all along that the fates would fuck with her. So now, fuck them all! Fuck the friends who dropped away when she was no longer one half of a couple. Fuck the deadbeats who didn't pay their outstanding bar tabs. Fuck L'America with its false promises of happiness and eternal love. She was forty-three years old. She had three children and no skills besides cooking and cleaning. *Va fungool*—up your ass—or *che cazze*, the Italian version of "what the fuck" wasn't enough any longer. As for her life now, only the gut-punch Anglo-Saxon "fuck" would do.

For all those years prior to swearing in English, Ma's vulgarity in Italian had been disguised by dialect, however harsh. During our battleground years, it was as if she were the teenager, always one-upping me, getting away with muttered remarks that never failed to enrage, even though I didn't know until years later what she was actually saying. The tone, however, was unmistakable. Her standard answer to my asking her where, for example, my schoolbag was would be something low and gargled like "*mezza le gosh*," which sounded filthy and gutterish and somehow sexual to my prissy ears. I later discovered that I was on the right track: *mezza le gosh* meant "between my thighs" in her dialect version of the Italian word *cosce*.

After Ma's conversion to the coarser but somehow less overtly sexual Anglo-Saxon curses, she had evolved them into a routine. In my twenties, home from New York for a visit with one of my girlfriends, my mother would smile, look her up and down, and ask: "You gotta boyfriend? No? How come? You a beautiful girl." Without waiting for a response, she would bring up the punch line. "I tell you why: all men are assaholes!" Then she would bark her signature laugh. More often than not, I joined in, only mildly discomfited by the English swear words that were never a part of my early childhood memories. But I still hushed and stifled her like a priggish schoolmarm, correcting her English, trying to disappear her in public. It wasn't that I myself didn't use the foulest of epithets every single day, especially in rageful rants about politics, misogyny, and blown auditions—I was an artist at blue vernacular. But I had a filter for polite company and the presence of "old" people that my mother didn't seem to register.

"Someday your children will make you suffer the way you make me suffer."

Ma hurled this invective at me so many times during my mean-girl phase that I was sure it would come true, like a looming curse from a bad fairy. Ma was witchy; she had prescient dreams and knew how to inflict *fatture*—hexes—on people.

And then my only son was born ten weeks early, and my mother's curse came true. I suffered with a burning, raw anguish to see him kept alive by tubes, his tiny chest fluttering with the delicacy and desperation of a hummingbird caught in a net.

On the third day of his life, when my son coded blue while my husband and I were in the neonatal intensive care unit, we both suffered, my husband along for the heart-stopping and hellish ride, collateral damage from my mother's curse. And if my husband was victim of a spillover hex, what did that make our Jesse, the personification of innocence who grew up to be quadriplegic and nonverbal and brilliant?

It made him a curse breaker, a conduit of unconditional love. And the one my mother and I had been waiting for all our lives without knowing it, the luminous being who told a story without words that we could both understand and agree on, the one who got us to communicate at last, mother to mother.

It wasn't that I had out-Pietà-ed her, and that Ma finally gave up trying to best me in the martyr derby—and it was more than a truce, what Jesse brought us. It was a lasting peace, a pact sworn in silence and compassion, in the place where words no longer mattered.

Holiday Shores

"Honey, I could go for somethin' good." This was Auntie Ellie's signal to Uncle Benny to go for a run to Jay's Drive-In before the late, late movie began. That meant big, greasy, delicious onion rings to go along with Bette Davis on television and staying up as late as I wanted. I was eight years old and spending the whole summer with my aunt and uncle, like I had every year since I was four. When I was at home with Ma during the school year, the nagging about bedtime began around seven thirty, while it was still light outside. Why couldn't I just live here forever, with my aunt and uncle? I often felt a pang of disloyalty to Ma and Daddy when this thought crossed my mind. But it always passed with the arrival of the onion rings.

The only time I was ever involved in a love triangle, it was chaste, but passionate, and it lasted for years. The threesome was composed of my aunt Ellie, my mother, and me. I had two mothers and no contest as to the winner of my affections.

Ellie always won. How could she not? She was summer personified: the beach, staying up late, the drive-in, the July 4th bonfire, all taking place in a dreamlike setting of sun and salt and laughter, in a place that was actually called "Holiday Shores."

When I bounded giddily into the backseat of Auntie Ellie and Uncle Benny's car, it was always the first Sunday after the end of the school year. I was going to live with them in their house by the sea for the whole summer and hope that summer would never end. I would see my father and mother only on weekends, when they and about thirty other friends drove down from our Boston suburb in a caravan of Chevys to spend the day at Holiday Shores. Auntie Ellie and Uncle Benny shared thirteen acres of land, a bay-side rocky beach, and a two-hundred-year-old house with Uncle Benny's younger brother, Johnny, and his wife, Camille, who lived downstairs. There was a big empty field beside their house on Main Street and on it was a huge billboard advertising "Holiday Shores," a beach with picnic tables, showers, and restrooms, all for ninety-nine cents per carload. A giant bathing beauty lolled in the forefront of the billboard against a false-advertising open ocean beach with sandy shores and huge waves. Auntie Ellie smoked in the front seat while I daydreamed in the back as Uncle Benny drove his old gray bomber down Route 128, my road to freedom. I looked forward to reading the stack of *True Romance* magazines piled in the bathroom, going to the drive-in every time the bill changed— Uncle Benny's company had supplied the cement blocks for the drive-in, so we breezed past the ticket booth shouting "Kingston Block," and were waved along like celebrities—and listening in on Camille and Auntie Ellie's grown-up conversations every morning when they took their coffee break. There were wild raspberries and blackberries growing alongside the dirt road to the beach, and the kid next door had a tree house, something I had only read about in books. And, my childhood Holy Grail: there was a barn with a hayloft and a stack of ancient magazines from the turn of the century, just the place to lose an entire afternoon in the musty pages of yesteryear. Best of all, there was a rustic boathouse right on the rocky beach with weathered gray shingles and a giant sliding door that had been built to move the boats in and out. Inside, there was a kitchen and old sofas and chairs, slightly musty from their proximity to the water. It was a huge single room, with one tiny other room, perfect for changing out of wet bathing suits. There were picnic tables outside, and Uncle Benny had built a wooden raft that the older kids used to dive off and jostle each other, pretending to push the girls into the icy green water. At low tide, the beach became a vast plain of mud, with huge seaweed-covered rocks giving the bay the appearance of a movie set for a dream world where dinosaurs still roamed. The awkward horseshoe crabs, living fossils moving in a counter-intuitive shuffle, added to the lost-world look of the beach at low tide. We slogged through the ankle-deep mud, squealing happily and on the hunt for quahogs. We watched for the little blowholes that gave away their hiding places, then dug for treasure. Ellie stuffed the oversized clams and baked them, and we kids felt like heroes and providers when she placed one before us, sizzling and delicious, filled with bread crumbs, parsley, and grated cheese and topped off with a crisp slice of bacon.

Ellie brought magic to my life. Ma brought rules.

Ellie treated me like a grown-up by showing me how to do things: how to hang clothes on a line, how to set a table, how to dust the stairs. I did these chores eagerly at her house. In my house, Ma did everything, but resented me for doing nothing in a circle game I could never win. Ellie let me listen in on adult conversations (as long as I was quiet); Ma sent me away or spoke Italian when things got interesting and adult. Uncle Benny took for granted that I would be okay water-skiing or rowing a boat or diving off the raft; Ma hovered whenever I did anything physical, on the alert for disaster and imminent death. Ellie handed me the antique key to the house and sent me from the boathouse up the dirt road in the dark to retrieve a pan or forgotten pack of cards or cigarettes. I was so frightened on my perilous journey that my breath came in gasps both going and coming back, but I felt triumphant on my return, as if I had circled the globe or outwitted leering fairy-tale trolls. I felt the same surge of confidence after I swam out to the raft on my own at Uncle Benny's prompting or learned the now-arcane skill of ironing his T-shirts. Ellie was amused at the things I said and delighted by the rapt attention I paid in turn to her stories. My mother often looked at me like I was an annoying door-to-door salesman and would lose patience almost immediately if I prattled on about school or books, swatting me out of the room like a fly buzzing too close to her family's food. I squirmed out of my mother's smothering embrace, but I stood open-mouthed and transfixed while Ellie ran her long red fingernails up and down the tender inside flesh of my arms, raising goosebumps.

But I still cried for my mother on the first night I slept away from her. I hid my tears from Ellie because I really wanted to stay. At the same time, I wanted the familiar: Ma, even if she did always sigh in that martyred way when I plucked timidly at her nightgown after yet another dream involving the tortures of the saints or apparitions of the Blessed Virgin Mary that had startled me awake. The apparitions may have seemed harmless or even a mark of favor to the child observers at Fatima or Lourdes on first glance, but I was only too aware, due to my obsessive reading of saint biographies, that two out of three of the Fatima kids who saw apparitions of the BVM died while they were children, and Saint Bernadette didn't live to a ripe old age either. Night after night I lay awake squinting at the corner of my bedroom: was that a faint blue glimmer I saw? The Virgin Mary didn't appear in the corner of my room at my aunt and uncle's house. I thought maybe it was because of the eaves that bent the ceiling so close to my bed in a protective slant. The BVM would have had to crouch, and that wasn't the way she rolled in the pictures and movies I had seen. She needed lots of room to float, standing upright, and a sizeable amount of space for the cherubs and the clouds and the rest of her heavenly entourage.

I was safe from the Blessed Mother, but still felt a longing for my own, a longing I didn't understand, because if Ma had magically appeared, trailing her dark aura, I would have turned my back on her and let my aunt spirit me back to the laughing place that was her everyday realm. Despite my nocturnal tears, I didn't rush up to my mother and father when they arrived with their caravan of friends on Sunday mornings. I hung back amid the babble of shouted greetings and raucous laughter as if I had been fostered out, the unwanted stepchild. I only moved nearer when my father called me, thrilled and suddenly shy at the sound of his voice.

Ma and Ellie were like sisters, not sisters-in-law. They shared power in a seesaw way, Ellie in control sometimes, and other times Ma on top. I never once saw the exchange of harsh words between them, in a relationship that lasted over sixty years. But there were subtle shifts and navigations through the shoals of family life. Ellie, though younger, was American born and able to negotiate simple things like doctors' instructions and school registrations, sailing through the officialdom that made Ma timid and querulous. Ma, though an immigrant, was married to Ellie's revered big brother who was like a father to her. Ma was also the better cook and queen for a day during holidays, always held at our house where my father sat at the head of the table. I wasn't the fulcrum of their power struggle. I was more like an imp that took turns sitting on each shoulder, along for the ride.

The defining tragedy in Ellie's life was her inability to have children. "I have an infantile womb," she told me when I was a little older than eight (but not by much). I pictured a badly behaved, psychotic toddler living in her nether regions, shouting "NO!" and strangling her babies to be. Ellie went on to describe a grisly-sounding operation she had to "stretch out her womb." Before the operation she had been pregnant three times and had lost three baby boys. She described Uncle Benny burying the tiny corpses in a shoebox and weeping bitterly. After the operation, though, she never became pregnant again. "They ruined me," she said.

So Auntie Ellie claimed me, and my brother (the greater prize) belonged to Ma.

In every holiday photograph, I am in Ellie's lap and Ma holds my brother. Everyone smiles in the photographs. There are no overt hostilities, ever. There is never an actual tug of war, just a war of attrition. I switch sides when it's convenient, like a corrupt ambassador representing the land of feckless youth. When Ellie tells tales of my mother's timidity handling me as an infant, and Ellie's own fearlessness, I smile and encourage more stories of Ma's ineptitude. When Ma calls home and pretends to be Ellie's prisoner at a night of bingo—Ma hates all games except the mental ones of her own devising—I laugh appreciatively at her fake-crying over the phone and pretend to agree that Ellie is acting like a tyrant by forcing her to go.

When my father died young, both my mother and Ellie were devastated. A few years later, Uncle Benny bowed out of a planned tour to Italy so that the two of them could team up, Lucy and Ethel on a Roman adventure. Instead of stomping grapes, they pounded a path to both my father's and mother's villages, boarding trains, hiring strangers to drive them to remote areas, and giggling like teenagers while they pretended to be clueless American tourists, then blindsided shop-owners with their rapid-fire Italian in a juicy dialect that proved they were not tourists at all. Poring over the photo album from the trip, they one-upped each other with mock insults. Ellie pointed to a picture of Ma, with her teased blonde hair and pantsuit, sitting with a roomful of ancient-looking crones. "Those are her girlfriends," Ellie snickered. "She got out just in time!" Ma showed a picture of Daddy's family, pointing to a stern-looking hillock of a woman. "That's the one everyone thought Ellie look like," she said, "'er cousin." She smiled back at Ellie, triumphant for the moment. Until Ellie pointed out how much Ma exaggerated the size of the piazza in her town. They went on in their teeter-totter fashion, thoroughly enjoying the re-hash of their trip and their ancient one-up game.

There were times when Ellie and Ma abandoned the seesaw and ran together like she-wolves. This was usually when one of us was threatened in some way. Some months after my father died, I committed the mortal sin of talking in class. The nun kept me after school and told me I'd been "running wild since my father died." (If only that nun could've seen what the university years would bring.) She was a smug, stolid little prig who liked to make her victims grovel. She threatened and scolded until I was in tears, and I didn't cry easily then; sullen silence and avoidance was my preferred MO for surviving parochial school. I told my mother. She and Ellie flew to the convent like avenging angels and landed like harpies upon the unfortunate nun. There were no visible signs of the attack the next day in class, but I was left alone from then on and the nun-bully kept her distance.

Our entwined lives went on, the triangle never shifting even after Ellie adopted two children, and my own son was born. I was there when Ma and Ellie drew their last breaths, as they were present when I drew my first. They died within a year of each other, as if the need to stay in touch went beyond their daily phone calls. I miss being on the seesaw end of one or the other when they spoke. I knew their routines so well I could fill in what I couldn't hear when I was at Ellie's or home with my mother, a sort of absurdist theater via *The Honeymooners* where the script never varied.

MA: Elenuh? [Fill in the blank] died.
ELLIE: Oh my God. D'ja go? How did she look?
MA: Good. An' she suffered before she die.
ELLIE: Yah. Andrew does a nice job. [Andrew Magni, the funeral director]
MA: Yah. Everybody came. The line was out the door.
ELLIE: Listen to this: Rita's daughter asked Santa Claus for bologna and cookies. (outraged) Bologna and cookies!
MA: Whatsamatter with 'er? That's stupida. The mother no feed?
ELLIE: (grimly) She feeds her, all right. All the time.
MA: (sighs) Eh. I dunno.

ELLIE: What was the number?

MA: (dolorously) Three-forty-two.

ELLIE: Off by one friggin' number! Son of a bitch!

MA: (echoing) Sominabitch.

They both sigh, their coda signaling the end of another conversation.

I never hear from them now, even in dreams, though they both boasted of their witchy powers when they were alive, and Ma threatened to haunt me on more than one occasion. But then my sister e-mails a recently discovered photograph of the two of them. By their swishy dresses and strappy shoes, I date the picture to be from the early fifties. The picture brings them back to me as surely as a haunting.

Ma and my aunt Ellie stand outside of Our Lady Help of Christians Church on a late spring day. They are dressed for a wedding in clothes I lust for today. I have a brief fantasy of strutting into an event wearing one of those retro dresses, until I remember the organ-crushing corseting that went on underneath. A vivid memory of Ma's vise-like girdle floats across my mind from the torture-device file where it has been stored. But in this picture she and Ellie are the height of glamour. Ma is wearing white gloves, strappy heels, and a light-colored, full-skirted dress. My aunt wears a black velvet V-necked top over a swishy black-satin skirt. A thin belt emphasizes her tiny waist. She also wears sexy high-heeled shoes. They both smile for the camera; my mother avoids a direct stare at the photographer, but Ellie looks right at the camera, head lifted as if daring someone to deny her beauty. Ma is in her early forties, Ellie in her late thirties. Ellie's hair is a halo of curls. My mother's is shorter, but just as curly. They both wear dark-red lipstick. They don't wear hats, and this is a mystery. In the background you can see glimpses of other women and men; all wear hats. My memory of Catholic Church even in the early sixties was that you didn't enter without covering your head, as a mark of respect. Even

a tissue bobby-pinned to your head would do if you forgot your hat. This photo is from the early to mid-fifties, but the hats are missing. Did they just brazen it out in church during the wedding, their hatless state? Granted, not wearing a hat to church in the fifties didn't have the dire consequences of leaving your burka behind to go to market in some Taliban backwater today, but still, there would have been looks, and maybe whispers. I don't think they cared. I can see them, side by side at Ma's dresser, getting ready for the wedding. They are looking in the mirror, Ellie maybe trying on one of those scalp-biting fifties hats that fit over your skull like earphones with teeth.

> ELLIE: Look what this is doin' to my hair. I look like Bozo the Clown.
> MA: (applying lipstick) Eh. Don' wear then.
> ELLIE: It's givin' me a headache.
> MA: (shrugs) Don' wear.
> ELLIE: It's not Mass; it's only a wedding.
> MA: Eh.
> ELLIE: Are you wearin' a hat?
> MA: Whadda you care? They lookin' at the bride, not you.
> ELLIE: Yeah. But they'll look at us, too.
> MA: Yeah.
> ELLIE: They bettah.
> *They both laugh and leave without hats.*

Ma's Rules for the Church

Q. How shall we know the things which we are to believe?

A. We shall know the things which we are to believe from the Catholic Church, through which God speaks to us.

    —BALTIMORE CATECHISM

Q. Which are the chief commandments of the Church?

A. The chief commandments of the Church are six:

1. To hear Mass on Sundays and holy days of obligation.
2. To fast and abstain on the days appointed.
3. To confess at least once a year.
4. To receive the Holy Eucharist during the Easter time.
5. To contribute to the support of our pastors.
6. Not to marry persons who are not Catholics, or who are related to us within the third degree of kindred, nor privately without witnesses, nor to solemnize marriage at forbidden times.

I memorized all the rules of the church in the Baltimore Catechism when I was seven. I had recently received my First Holy Communion. Holy Communion is a sacrament of the church. A

split second after I received first Holy Communion, the Catholic Church held me liable for my sins because I had attained the age of reason and was supposed to know right from wrong. I knew that missing Sunday Mass, even one, damned you to an eternity of fiery torment in hell, with no escape possible. It was a mortal sin, the kind that couldn't be wiped away by anything but a priest's absolution in the confessional box. If you slipped off a curb and were creamed by a delivery truck on the way to confession, woe betide you, as my first-grade teacher, Sister Juventius, said often and with the self-satisfied relish of the righteous. Eternal torment in the lake of fire would be your fate, and even though you had intended to go to confession, tough for you; it didn't count. That was the rule. Sister Juventius was adamant, like her Christian martyr namesake, who refused to break the rule about honoring relics as ordered by the emperor and was flayed alive and beheaded as a result. There were no exceptions. Ever. Missing Mass on Sunday was a mortal sin. This was a Rule of the Church.

My mother, the previous source of all wisdom and authority before Sister Juventius, was flirting with the fires of hell. She never went to Mass on Sunday. Instead she spent every Sunday morning pouring a huge mound of flour onto the kitchen table, breaking egg after egg into the hollowed-out center she made, then kneading the yellow dough into what became the spaghetti we had every Sunday for dinner. Even though Ma irritated me by making me wear snow pants under my school uniform on cold days and refusing to let me stay up late to watch old movies on television, I didn't want her to burn. I didn't want to be separated from my mother for all eternity (this sentiment would change drastically in a few short years when I reached adolescence). I was planning to follow all the rules and go to heaven and be with God. And I wanted my mother to be there with me. Strangely, I never worried about my father. The only thing he did with religious zeal every Sunday morning was play golf. In the winter he played poker instead of going to church. But I thought—no, I was *sure* that he was so charming and outgoing, he would talk his way in, no problem. He owned a bar and had devoted followers. I saw no reason why God shouldn't be one of them.

Ma, on the other hand, was volatile. She didn't have the patience to be charming. She could hurl a kitchen implement in a flash, and before you ever knew she had lost her temper, you were ducking flying wooden spoons or colanders, and you found yourself impaled on the spiky points of her Italian dialect as she screeched, *"Che ti possan'uccidere'!"* Loosely translated as "I hope they kill you!" Ma wouldn't take direct responsibility for the killing. It would be some murky, anonymous "they" who would perform the deed, presumably at her bidding.

The most direct threats of murder always came during dinner because I hated almost every food group. This horrified my family. My father grew up hungry. My aunt Ellie told me a story about my father as a little boy balking at some dinner my grandmother made. They were alone together for ten years in the impoverished mountain village of San Donato, waiting for my grandfather to make enough money in America to send for them. My father complained. My grandmother said nothing. She sat across from him and continued to eat her meager supper. When she finished, she reached across for my father's plate and ate his food, every bite, without saying a word. He never complained again.

I am sure this story was told to me as a cautionary tale. Instead, it worked in reverse. When I was my father's age in the story, around ten, I would have dearly loved for someone to reach across and take away my plate and finish my dinner for me, because it was likely that I hated what was on it. I found almost all food repulsive, a living blasphemy to my parents who grew up where food was hard-won and, therefore, holy.

My mother's sacred rule about bread was that it was always to be handled with reverence, because when you store it upside down or show any kind of disrespect to this source of life, God cries.

I didn't care if God sobbed. I didn't like my chicken to touch my broccoli. Eggs in any form had a fatal relationship to snot and were therefore untouchable and impossible to look at much less put anywhere near my mouth. The texture of mashed potatoes made me gag. Milk was poison. Luckily, my mother agreed with me on this one. She served orange soda with our macaroni when we had it on Sundays and Wednesdays. She believed the combination of milk and tomato sauce could be lethal, which made sense to me. The only food that I didn't find revolting was my mother's hand-cut spaghetti and meatballs and the meatless lentil soup she made for Fridays that also contained the hand-cut noodles.

Weekday dinners were a test for any future saint, and I considered myself one, a would-be saint suffering torture tests from God. It wasn't just about the food. I couldn't stand the sound of my grandfather's slurping when eating the weekday macaroni. I hated my little sister's tiny mouse bites, the gnawing and crackling of crusts with her sharp baby teeth. I wanted to kill my little brother for the sneaky way he opened his mouth so that only I could see his dinner, exposing his chewed-up food and making me recoil in disgust as if he were an old pervert shaking his junk at me in a doorway. I tried to withstand these torments, like Saint Lawrence, who was burned on a giant griddle, like a piece of French toast, and when he was done on one side, asked to be flipped over to the other. I used comic books at the table for distraction. I buried my nose in *Tales from the Crypt* during meals, but the animal sounds of grunting and slurping would inevitably break through, and then I would have to look, like a rubbernecker at a fatal accident. I succumbed every time. I complained, louder and louder until my mother threatened me with the knife she was using to carve the round, sacred Italian loaf held against her chest, the artisanal bread from Magni's Bakery that foodies would rhapsodize over today.

"I got a knife in my 'an," she would say, pointing it at me, her voice low and deadly, the Cockney ring to her dropped aitches making me smirk, enraging her further. I went back to my comic book, but at the next loud burble from grandpa I started up again,

with louder complaints and full-body shivers of disgust. Finally,
Ma would scream at me to get out before they killed me ("*Che
ti possan'uccidere'!*"), and I would take my comic book and go to
my room, triumphant, the half-eaten food on my plate left behind,
a wordless rebuke to my mother, who could take some comfort
in the fact that she would eat her own dinner later, in the dining
room, in the company of only my father and a glass of homemade
red wine.

Maybe the rules were different in southern Italy, where Ma was
born. She was certainly cavalier in brushing off my tearful warnings about the eternal fire. Usually, she laughed and told me that
God didn't require mothers to go to Mass on Sundays; it was much
more important to get the pasta ready for Sunday dinner. I watched
her wield the long, dangerous-looking *tackeril* to roll out the dough
thin as a sheet of paper. She wasn't even dressed for Mass. She
didn't look anything like the pictures of mothers in my catechism.
They all wore pastel-colored shirtwaist dresses and little flowery
hats. I don't think Ma owned a shirtwaist. She wore blood-red lipstick and snug-fitting black Capri pants that accentuated her lush
figure. Not for Ma the frilly aprons I saw on housewives in '60s
magazine ads. My mother wore, barman-style, a *moppina* (dishtowel) tucked into her waist and another one slung rakishly over
her shoulder as she rolled the leathery-looking pasta dough into a
log, swiftly sliced off the noodles, then hung them up to dry.

Q. *Are we bound to honor and obey others than our parents?*
A. We are also bound to honor and obey our bishops, pastors,
    magistrates, teachers, and other lawful superiors.

I didn't dare ask Sister Juventius about Ma's rules. Somehow
I sensed that the anticipation and enjoyment of spaghetti wasn't
an excuse. I don't think Sister Juventius ever ate spaghetti for
Sunday dinner. The few times I had been to the convent on errands, it had smelled faintly of boiled meat and cabbage, which

was what I suspected the nuns ate every day, including Sunday. If Ma left meat boiling in a pot until it turned gray, she would have time to go to Mass. But here's where I was complicit in Ma's sin: I didn't want gray meat for Sunday dinner. I wanted, craved, loved with a love bordering on the profane, her hand-cut spaghetti, even though I knew it made me an accomplice in the blackening of her soul. Ma's homemade Sunday spaghetti could perform miracles: one bite put me into a fugue state that allowed me to transcend my misophonia and silence other people's noises at the table, the same ones that during weekday meals incited skirmishes and murderous threats. Ma's Sunday spaghetti erased all that; even my little brother's open-mouthed reveals couldn't pierce the glow of well-being that began with that bowl placed before me. Still, the nagging aura of blasphemy hovered faintly over Ma's spaghetti like tainted steam. Wasn't this the way I was supposed to feel when the priest laid the Host that represented Jesus on my tongue at Sunday Mass? That feeling of euphoria at receiving the Body of Christ never happened during the rite of Holy Communion. There was only the memory of the nun's warnings not to tamper with the Host, to swallow reverently, bow your head, and go back to your pew. But the Host, a white paper-thin piece of unleavened bread, often stuck to your upper palate in a gluey God-meld that could last for what felt like days, as the minutes ticked by and you tried to work your tongue (always in a respectful way) to loosen God so you could swallow Him. Touching the Host was out of the question; we had been warned about committing that unthinkable sacrilege by Sister Juventius. One evil boy, she told us, sneaked out of the church, took the Host out of his mouth, and stabbed It with a pencil. The devilish boy was later found dead with holes around his heart that looked just like pencil marks. Even using your tongue to pry God loose was suspect, but until He was swallowed, Ma's spaghetti would have to wait. This is the reason I spent most of the Mass with my face contorted, eyes blinking in distress, and

mouth pursed—in a frantic effort to gobble the Body of Christ so
I could clear the way for Ma's spaghetti.

Q. *How do the priests of the Church exercise the power of forgiving sins?*
A. The priests of the Church exercise the power of forgiving sins by
hearing the confession of sins and granting pardon for them as
ministers of God and in His name.

Ma never went to confession, and without confession and absolution by a priest, her soul would remain as black as the draw-
ings of sinful souls in my catechism. These haunting illustrations
showed the consequences of sin: a hollowed-out picture of a man
and woman whose insides held only blackness, an absence of divine light, sticky and poisonous and impossible to remove, like
years and years of burned-on oven grease. I showed Ma the pictures of her soul, but they didn't scare her at all. In fact, she hardly
looked at them, her hands plunged into a sinkful of squid carcasses
that would become stuffed calamari; she never broke rhythm from
pulling the tentacled squid heads away from their slippery white
bodies.

Q. *How should Christians look upon the priests of the Church?*
A. Christians should look upon the priests of the Church as the
messengers of God and the dispensers of His mysteries.

"What, I gotta tell my sins to some *guy*? Aaaaay," she said, flick-
ing her hand under her chin and spraying me with a fine mist of
squid guts. I screamed and shuddered, backing away. My mother
laughed and called me "Miss Prim," a label I hated but had to
admit was true. I would rather be stabbed through the throat like
Saint Cecilia than touch anything slimy. I was a *schifosa* of the
first order, someone who found almost everything repulsive, even
beyond my storied hatred of food. I feared babies and their leak-
ages, insects of every kind, and even my own scabby knees. It was

Ma's fake wedding portrait

Birth announcement

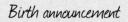

Ma's Mother, Maria Domenica, "unsmiling,
inky eyes wide, her misery palpable"

Ma's Father, Gaetano, "be happy, otherwise
the people laugh at you"

Ma + Dad + me

guillotine slanted bangs,
bad Tonette perm,
jack o'lantern teeth—
first grade portrait

Archangel Michael, just before my attempted assassination of him by peanut

First Holy Communion and first bad acting attempt at faking reverence

Ma and Aunt Ellie: brazen, hatless women

Nice, like a prostitute

My father, behind the bar at Leone's Café

Ma's haunted picture

Ma with Jesse

Ma and me later

Ma speaks up

because I was destined to be a saint, I told myself. I was not of this world. My mother agreed, often telling me I didn't belong to this family, or even this planet. But I felt compelled to correct my mother's impression of priests.

"It's not some *guy*, Ma; it's a priest! They're like God here on Earth. That's what Sister Juventius says!"

"*Che cazze.* Sister Juventius. Like God, huh? I'm tellin' you somethin' now: the nuns don' know everything! When I was a little girl, you' age in Italy, the priest was late for Mass one day. They send me to get 'im, an' I come back and tell the people: 'He's playin' horsey with the housekeeper!'"

At this point she laughed loudly, her signature seal-bark laugh, and I wondered what the joke was. The priest was late for Mass? So that's why she won't go to confession and wipe clean her soul? I was confused. And the priest wasn't a "guy." He was God's anointed representative on Earth. Wasn't he allowed to play horsey? "Guys" didn't have the magical power to remove the stain of sin and bestow blessings, only priests. Of course, I didn't say any of this. I just stared uncomprehendingly at my mother, whose laughter began to ebb as she looked at me, probably wondering how she had produced this skinny, worried creature with lopsided bangs and a bad Tonette perm. Finally she shrugged her shoulders, pushed back a rebellious lock of her raven's-wing hair, and with a "beh" went back to gutting the squid.

Maybe she was just crazy and God would forgive her.

Q. *Is it right to show respect to the pictures and images of Christ and His saints?*

A. It is right to show respect to the pictures and images of Christ and His saints, because they are the representations and memorials of them.

I had an irrational hope that Ma's huge collection of religious artifacts might buy her clemency with God. She had a Virgin of

Fatima lamp that represented the three devoted little kids who had
first spotted the Holy Mother. In the lamp version the kids were
praying around a light bulb at Mary's feet. Ma had a dress-up Baby
Jesus, an Infant of Prague statue with his own seasonal wardrobe,
red-and-white robes for everyday wear, purple for Lent, and mauve
for Advent. She had statues of Saint Francis, Saint Anthony, Saint
Jude, and the Virgin Mary, and she lit votive candles to them when
they came across with a winning lottery number. Sometimes,
though, she punished them by turning their faces to the wall.
When I was four, the German shepherd next door almost took my
eye out. Saint Francis spent a month facing the wall for that over-
sight. He was the patron saint of animals and clearly wasn't doing
his job. Ma was the God of her own universe, and the saints would
do time until her displeasure with them was relieved by an answer
to one of her profane prayers.

Q. *What is forbidden by the Second Commandment?*
A. The Second Commandment forbids all false, rash, unjust, and
    unnecessary oaths, blasphemy, cursing, and profane words.

If Ma would say the ejaculations on the back of the holy card
Sister Juventius had given me, she could knock off years in purgatory, which was sort of a refugee camp on the way to heaven.
Every time you broke one of the rules, you had time added on to
your stay in the camp, even after the priest wiped the sin away in
confession. The card Sister Juventius had given me had a little pa-
renthesis after each expression that told you how many years the
holy ejaculation was worth. A "Sacred Heart of Jesus, I place my
trust in Thee" could get you three hundred days off. If you said it a
thousand times a day, you could get three hundred thousand days
off! But Ma wasted her time every day watching her soap opera,
Love of Life, on TV, and the only ejaculation she would say was "Jesus, Marianne, and Joseph!" at dinnertime or other times I vexed
her, dragging me into her blasphemy of the Lord's name. At the

rate she was going, purgatory, the way station to heaven, wasn't even an option. No, Ma was going straight to hell.

I developed facial tics from trying to follow all the rules. I kept blinking my eyes and clearing my throat, causing Ma to mutter, "Jesus, Marianne, and Joseph," as she worried aloud about my sanity. I had nightmares every night. I would bolt awake from yet another dream about Saint John the Apostle boiling in a vat of oil or Saint Isaac Jogues having his fingers chewed off by Mohawks and lie awake knowing that I would give in and worship pagan idols the minute the pagans showed me an implement of torture. I would then, after agonizing deliberations alone in my room, creep into my parents' bedroom and tug on Ma's arm, waking her up, my weakness causing yet another sin of blasphemy. "Jesus, Marianne, and Joseph, I was havin' such a good dream!"

Q. *Why does the Church command us to abstain from flesh-meat on Fridays?*

A. The Church commands us to abstain from flesh-meat on Fridays, in honor of the day on which our Saviour died.

On Fridays, school lunch was always soggy fish sticks and a side vegetable: an ice-cream scoop of rock-hard mashed potatoes. At Our Lady Help of Christians Elementary School, the nuns hovered, gliding through the cafeteria as if on skates, hands disappeared into their voluminous sleeves. There was nothing lissome, however, about the way they could suddenly turn from skater to raptor and swoop down upon some picky eater. The nuns made sure children finished lunches, even if the weekday lunch was fried baloney, with grease pooling in pink rubbery folds, or gray, boiled mystery meat or soggy Friday fish sticks, even if the smell of lukewarm milk resulted in the smell of vomit from the kids who had been forced to drink the warm milk and eat the baloney, and had then immediately deposited the upchucked remains on the linoleum floor where they sat, awaiting Mr. Greeley the janitor, who covered the mess, which was indistinguishable from its previous incarnation as a hot lunch, with bright Kelly-green sawdust, reincarnating it as a hot lunch.

For Friday dinner, we fared much better at my house. The no-meat rule was, strangely, observed by Ma, and her signature Friday dish was a delicious lentil and tomato soup with her own hand-cut noodles. I couldn't figure out why she obeyed this particular rule of the church, since she never allowed anyone to dictate culinary matters at our house and was the undisputed queen and absolute ruler of the kitchen. Even when my two aunts pitched in during elaborate holiday dinners, they were more like her acolytes, scurrying to wash plates and chop vegetables at her bidding. Kids, like myself, were banned outright. If she wasn't following God's command to go to church every Sunday, she would never allow Him to tell her how to run her kitchen. The unusual adherence to the no-meat rule remained a mystery for years.

Q. *Do those who make use of spells and charms, or who believe in dreams, in mediums, spiritists, fortune-tellers, and the like sin against the First Commandment?*

A. Those who make use of spells and charms, or who believe in dreams, in mediums, spiritists, fortune-tellers and the like, sin against the First Commandment, because they attribute to creatures perfections which belong to God alone.

When I was in high school, I decided that all religion was claptrap. Ma pretended to be shocked and dismayed, but I knew that secretly she didn't care, as long as I continued to observe *her* rules about *her* religion. That meant never even acknowledging the existence of frozen vegetables or jarred tomato sauce, and obeying the milk-tomato sauce ban. It meant warding off death by calling it to you, jokingly, with a sneer in your voice, like when Ma would see a hearse drive by and say: "There's my new car." It meant paying close attention to dreams, in case a dead relative was trying to tell you something or bestow a favor, like giving you a number to play in the lottery. It meant learning to thwart the *malocchio* (evil eye) on Christmas Eve, Ma transferring her powers to me at midnight so she wouldn't lose her own, teaching me the chant in Italian, showing me how to break up the "eyes" that formed when you poured olive oil and salt into the blessed water with your witchy left hand. Most importantly, it meant hewing to Ma's rule as kitchen goddess, the Source of All That Is Delicious in the World. The Kitchen Rules trumped the rules about the *malocchio* or dreams or sneering at death. And Ma's hand-cut spaghetti trumped everything else.

At eighteen I left home and started school at the University of Massachusetts–Boston, working my way through with part-time shifts at Tarry 'n' Taste Donut Shop on Charles Street. I found my own apartment on the slummy side of Beacon Hill, shared with two equally clueless friends. None of us knew how to cook (or pay utilities, or hang curtains, or get the super when the refrigerator died). I lived on doughnuts and Carnation Instant Breakfast until my body began to scream like the soundtrack from *Psycho*. I broke down and ate a hamburger every day for lunch. I considered this a balanced diet. Did I mention I was smoking a lot of weed at the time?

The next year, I became a college sophomore cliché by going on a macrobiotic diet. Now my new roommate, Maria, and I had a regimen of only brown rice, seaweed, tofu, and miso soup. We ate vegetables, except for tomatoes (we learned that they belonged to the deadly nightshade plant family). All this information was gleaned from our new food bible: *You Are All Sanpaku*, by George Ohsawa. The book told us to check our eyes; if you could see white under the iris, it meant you were already half dead, that your eyes were rolling up like a corpse's. Maria and I each had big brown eyes with plenty of white showing below the iris, possibly because we were in the habit of constantly rolling them. That thought never occurred to us, though, in the grips of *sanpaku* fever. After staring at our eyes side by side in the cramped bathroom mirror, we agreed—we were both definitely, dangerously *sanpaku*.

On a weekend visit home, my mother reacted to the tomato ban with the glazed horror of someone living under twenty-four-hour bombardment. Now her daughter's food loathing had spread to every food group like an unchecked plague germ, engulfing the previously exempt spaghetti and meatballs and tomato-lentil soup. But I was no innocent plague victim. I had *chosen* to eat tofu and seaweed, spurning her spaghetti and meatballs with cold indifference. Ma stood there, mute with contempt, as I sat before the Sunday dinner, not touching her food, unpacking my plastic container of brown rice and seaweed. I explained the concept of *sanpaku*, between puffs of my cigarette—oh, yes, I continued to smoke throughout my new health regimen—figuring she'd at least like the rolled eye-corpse thing. My mother had been referring to me as *mezzo mort'* (half dead) my entire life, even though this was usually a lament about how much time I wasted lolling around reading. But my mother found no amusement in the fact that her daughter was finally acknowledging that she was half dead. She was too mortally insulted by the plastic container of seaweed and brown rice sitting on the table like a stool sample, profaning her tomato sauce, defiling her kitchen.

I didn't cook during my university years, except to make brown rice and seaweed for my year-that-was-like-a-century-long macrobiotic diet. When I finally began to cook and called asking for recipes, she was vague and left things out—on purpose, it seemed. I gave up asking Ma for recipes and instead consulted my aunt Ellie and Italian cookbooks. Ma's recipes for hand-cut pasta and her lentil soup were lost forever, I thought, when she died, suddenly, in 2004.

Q. *What is a mystery?*
A. A mystery is a truth which we cannot fully understand.

A year and a half after my mother died, my husband and I and a couple of friends went to a tiny restaurant in a teeming alleyway off the main streets of Naples, Italy. There were no other Americans, just multigenerational Neapolitan families crowding the murky space, babies wailing, cutlery thrown to the table by busy waiters, the ebullient babble of southern dialect rising above the steaming pasta. The impatient waiter slammed *acqua gassata* and wine on the table and thrust his chin out, exasperated, waiting for our order. I got the lentil soup.

Upon my first mouthful of the soup, I surprised my tablemates by bursting into tears. It was the lentil soup of my childhood, the lentil soup of all those meatless Fridays, the lentil soup I had tried and failed many times to make, the soup I thought I'd never taste again after my mother died. My friend Maggie asked for a taste. She lifted her spoon and savored the soup. Then she sat back and smiled. "You know why you could never figure out the recipe? There's meat in the soup. It's pork, I think." I tasted it again. She was right.

I suddenly heard my mother's voice, clearly: "Whadda those priests know about making a soup? You ken' make a good soup without meat! So, I put it in, I take it out, okay; now it'sa soup you ken eat on Friday."

Only she never took it out. There were the hair-like pork strands, visibly floating in the broth, just like they had done in Ma's Friday soup. I just never saw them.

Grace After Meals.

We give Thee thanks for all Thy benefits, O Almighty God, who livest and reignest for ever; and may the souls of the faithful departed, through the mercy of God, rest in peace.

Amen.

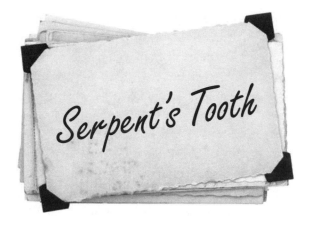

Serpent's Tooth

If she must teem,
Create her child of spleen; that it may live
And be a thwart disnatur'd torment to her!
Let it stamp wrinkles in her brow of youth;
With cadent tears fret channels in her cheeks;
Turn all her mother's pains, and benefits,
To laughter and contempt; that she may feel
How sharper than a serpent's tooth it is
To have a thankless child!
—King Lear, Act 1, Scene 4

During my relentlessly hostile teen years, my mother, the bulls-eye on my rancor target, drew solace from her grim companions onscreen, the bitter all-star *maters dolorosa* of late-night melodrama. This band of mothers was headed by Joan Crawford as Mildred Pierce and Juanita Moore as Annie, Lana Turner's African American maid in *Imitation of Life*. Both of them had bad daughters, evil, snake-tongued ingrates who stabbed them again and again straight through the heart with their cold-blooded rejections and betrayals. Each mother had something to offer in the competition for the crown of thorns. Each one vied to be Queen of Anguish, the mother who had suffered most from her Bad Daughter. My mother felt she should be in the running, too, that our struggle was just as epic and she was just as martyred.

"Leave me alone! Stop telling people I'm your daughter! I'm not like *you*! I'm white!" screamed Annie's passing-for-white daughter, Sarah Jane (Susan Kohner in real life), to her wet-eyed, forgiving-to-the-point-of-being-a-doormat mother.

"You'll never be anything but a common frump whose father lived over a store and whose mother took in washing," spat snobby Ann Blyth as Vida, ingrate daughter of work-her-fingers-to-the-bone Mildred Pierce.

"Why don't you leave me alone and get back up on the cross where you love to be?" I said to my own sobbing mother, as cool as Vida, as raw as Sarah Jane, my delivery pure, calculated spite.

I remember the nails-on-chalkboard feeling the mere presence of my mother provoked in those years, as if my nerve endings were frayed electrical wires emitting sparks. Ugh, the way she talked, like the fat cartoon Italian waiter in *Lady and the Tramp*. Ugh, the way she chewed. Her indelicate nose (*my* nose). Her veiny legs (would mine get like that?). Ugh, her pointy breasts. I shivered with disgust. I fumed. I envied her breasts. I pictured her dead. No, no, just disappeared. I pictured her gone, gone back to Italy so she couldn't annoy me, gone so that I could be alone with my father. I belonged there, in the pantheon of Bad Daughters of the silver screen. I earned my place among my fellow teen devils without the need to study their ways; I came by my meanness naturally—it wasn't a stretch, a fact that chills me now. No wonder my poor mother needed those films as group therapy.

Imitation of Life and *Mildred Pierce* were the ur-soaps, and for Ma their draw became a siren call, gluing her to the set whenever they appeared on late-night movies or the afternoon offering, Boston Movietime. In the days before video recordings, those films only aired randomly, sometimes as if by conjure when my mother needed them enough and her inner *strega* took over, summoning them. Ma's regular daytime soaps, *The Secret Storm* and *Love of Life*, didn't satisfy, not at all. Oh, their pulsing organ scores and ominous title sequences promised dramatic eruptions, but they never delivered.

Nothing could top the gut-level pleasure of the last scene in *Imitation of Life*, where Sarah Jane throws herself on her mother's coffin, too late, too late, all her screaming affirmations of love for naught, her mother dead and gone forever. Sarah Jane fights her way through the crowd at her mother's funeral, shrieking the words her mother longed all her life to hear: "Let me through! I'm sorry! *That's my mother!*" Sarah Jane's tearful passion, her suicidal regret, her physical collapse all made visceral sense to my Italian mother. Where she came from, it was expected and customary to pull bodies out of coffins at funerals, to scream with outrage at death, to jump into open graves to be with your loved ones. The pallid daytime soaps were more like instruction manuals on how to be an American. On the daytimes, stories moved at a glacial pace, voices remained hushed and civil, disputes were resolved politely over coffee poured out of gleaming silver tea services inherited from Great-Aunt Edith. At our house, an ordinary Sunday dinner could end in death threats if one of the kids got too mouthy or ululating screams if someone announced the passing of some ninety-year-old, distantly related *paisan'*. It was opera, the stuff of La Scala, and the frenzied whispers and polite gasps of the citizens of Rosehill on daytime television were mere background noise for my mother's daily moment of Zen as she put up her feet and crocheted a new blanket, on a break from cleaning the house and cooking for my father's bar. Watching the "exciting story of Vanessa Dale and her courageous struggle for human dignity" on *Love of Life* must have resonated with my put-upon mother, even when it didn't reflect her own life, even if it wasn't exciting in the least. And the dialogue could be instructive. Lines like "I think you're some strange suffering demon sent back to earth to torture and be tortured" could have come in handy during one of our epic mother-daughter screaming fights, if only my mother could wrap her tongue around that impossible English phrasing. Instead, her wobbly English failed her in the crunch every time. She could only dream of compelling her tongue to perform with the same speed and precision as her crochet hook, darting in and out with machine-like, devastating efficiency.

"Leave me alone! Stop telling people I'm your daughter! I'm not like you."

I'm eleven years old. I'm walking home from Our Lady Help of Christians Elementary School, my green schoolbag slung over my shoulder, my knee socks bagging. It's an early spring afternoon, the kind that imbues everyone in New England with hope for about the two minutes they have between ice storms. I'm late getting home because I've stopped off at the library for another lives of the saints book. (I want desperately to be a saint. Hell looms large; sainthood is a safety hedge against the eternal flames.)

The day shift of the factory across the street from my house is getting out. A swarm of mostly women fans out onto the sidewalk surrounding our big yard, lush with flowers my father has planted, a grape arbor, a pear tree, and an apple tree. My mother is on her hands and knees on our lawn, dragging a colander full of dandelion leaves she's digging up for *insalata*. I love *cicoria*, but I wish our salad came from the A&P, cellophane wrapped and sanitary and American. A tough-looking woman, the grown-up version of the public school girls who threaten me regularly on the way home from school, regards my mother. "Hunting for Easter eggs," she says in a basso voice, exhaling smoke from her after-work cigarette. Her pig-nosed companion shrieks with laughter. I want to confront the women for mocking my mother. I wish my nose turned up like that laughing woman's. I'd even risk looking like a piglet if it made me look American. But most of all, I want to distance myself from this stranger's ridicule. "I don't eat weeds," I plan to say, my own adenoidal voice magically transformed into a film star's throaty warble. Instead, I walk by my house, pretending I don't live there, so the woman won't see me. I'm not like *her*, I tell myself. I'm not like that foreign woman on her knees, like a serf, like a common frump whose mother took in washing. I'm not like her. I'm *American*.

I spend my early teen years trying to dissociate myself from my mother. I even take on some of the characteristics of squeaky-cute Sandra Dee in *Imitation of Life*; in the film she falls in love with her mother's boyfriend. I dream of having my father all to myself, so we can read books together and discuss them. My mother never reads books and yells at me when I read: she is convinced I will go blind or crazy or both and that reading is just a way for me to get out of helping her around the house. My father has earned the right to read because he works. I disparage my mother's ignorance in what I think of as subtle hints about her illiteracy. I am utterly transparent, and my father ignores the hints and goes on being my father and her loving husband. My mother rubs it in by telling me: "Your father says I'm the best." There is no doubt what she means by "best." As usual, she has pushed it too far and I am totally disgusted and grossed out. "*Common*," I think in my Vida persona.

Years later, after the mother-daughter war had devolved into the odd skirmish at holidays or snippy retort during phone calls, my mother was able to indulge in a final wave of *schadenfreude*, thanks to my career choice: I became an actress. I never appeared on the daytimes (I was "too ethnic"). My only connection to the soaps was when, early in his career, my all-American actor husband robbed someone on *One Life to Live,* and thus funded our bare-bones honeymoon on Cape Cod.

In college, Ma came to see me play the role of Marica del Reino, an elderly widow, in *Divinas Palabras,* by Ramon del Valle-Inclan. An overwrought symbolic drama that involved nudity and onstage masturbation, *Divinas Palabras* was risky going at our state college, even in the late sixties, but our theater professor seemed to be unaware he was dealing with queasy nineteen-year-olds who had never acted before. Picture preschoolers staging Camus and you get the idea. My dramatic moment came when Marica's only nephew, a hydrocephalic, was "EATEN! EATEN BY PIGS!" the immortal lines I shrieked before collapsing into a quivering heap. I could feel my mother's beamed approval from the audience when I discovered the giant chewed, bloody plastic head of my stage nephew and emitted full-throated banshee wails. I knew that she felt like I had at last claimed my heritage. Finally, I belonged to my family.

But Marica del Reino was only the beginning; my DNA was radiating the martyr mother archetype to casting directors, and more distraught mothers were in my acting future.

My mother was transported when I was cast on *The Sopranos.* Not only did she get to crisscross the neighborhood asking the *whyos* at Dunkin's, the newspaper store guy, the bookies at the soccer club, and the elderly girls at her hair salon, "You watch-a *The Sopran's?*" she got to see her smart-mouth daughter transform into the role she had wished on me since my teens: I was now the mother of a thankless child. But there was one big problem: my child was a wayward son, not a bad daughter. In the series, my son, Christopher, was violent, addicted to drugs, and dating a girl I hated. My character, Joanne, was a rancorous alcoholic who felt outclassed by the wealthier members of her extended family, always getting the worst table at social events and having her cheap presents snickered over at a wedding shower for her despised future daughter-in-law. In the first scene I had with my son, he playfully noogied me, and sniffed my breath for alcohol. I had my hair in rollers and was wearing a pink chenille housecoat, plus dark eye-circle makeup and broken blood vessels drawn all over my nose (the drink). Any old boyfriend viewing the show could count himself lucky for getting out before my premature aging and alcoholic demise. But my mother thought my son, Christopher, was a good boy. Didn't he visit his mother? Didn't he leave me a twenty-dollar bill taped to the refrigerator?

By the end of my run as Christopher's mother, my television spawn had cursed me out during his intervention in language so blistering I didn't have to fake looking shocked, and in another episode, I hid in my apartment while thugs threatened me at the door and chased me down the street. My mother still made excuses for Christopher. She implied it was my fault somehow, and that Christopher's girlfriend was the bad influence. In my mother's worldview, men—husbands and sons—were to be cared for, as if they were incompetent. This was clear. After my father died and she was a young widow, she refused to consider remarrying. "What—I gotta take cayuh of some old man now?" was her rejoinder when asked about the possibility of dating. This is why sons were off the hook—they didn't know any better; they were custodial. Daughters were to be sparred with, to toughen them up for the harsh tasks that would lie ahead in life—taking care of sons and husbands and, possibly, "some old guy."

No wonder I put off getting married for years.

But when my son arrived I was grateful for my serpent's tongue and the teenage struggles for my own independence, my fight-to-the-death stubbornness. Most of all, I was thankful for my mother, my first, my toughest, and most loving adversary. And I'm lucky: I realized all this before she died, so that at her funeral I didn't have to reenact her favorite scene from *Imitation of Life*, with poor Sarah Jane flinging herself on her mother's coffin and declaring to the world that she was her mother's daughter when it was too late. In delivering her eulogy I was able to declare before the world without an operatic flourish, without remorse, but with the gratitude that was always hidden in my heart's core that she was my mother: warrior, *mater dolorosa*, sparring partner, teacher, and guide.

Nice, Like a Prostitute

I kept asking to see the balloon. I wanted the balloon. The pretty red-haired lady who lived in the little house next door was keeping it from me, hiding it under her skirt. She sat in my kitchen smiling and pretending to be nice. Why wouldn't she give me the balloon? Why was she being so mean? I started to whine. I tried to climb up under her skirt. My mother stopped me. "That's a baby in there," she said. "Not a balloon." The pretty red-haired lady was not the first pregnant woman I had seen, but it was somehow the first time I realized that babies were in there, not balloons. I asked my mother how the baby got out of the lady and she told me that God opened up your stomach when the time was right. I was four. In my world of flying monkeys, ghosts, and apparitions of the Blessed Virgin Mary, it all made sense. Why wouldn't God open up your stomach when the time was right? A little stomach opening was but a trifle compared to creating an entire universe. For years I pictured the birth process as animated and with goofy sound effects, all fueled by Saturday-morning cartoons and the tales of religious miracles I heard every day at school.

I was eight when I figured out what went where, thanks to my Nancy Drew–enhanced eavesdropping skills and the teenage girls recruited to walk me to church, since both my parents had better things to do on Sunday mornings. I was, like every other kid on the planet, disgusted and in denial when I heard about what my parents did at night and probably on Sunday mornings while I was being walked to church and, I now realized, on afternoons when business at my father's bar was slow. I had come home from school a few times a week to find my father sipping coffee in the kitchen with Ma, both of them connected in some new and weird way I couldn't fathom, bathed in what I didn't catch then but know now was afterglow.

By seventh grade, when most of my friends were budding and I remained tightly furled, our nun teachers had begun the long, mostly futile campaign to convince us that sex was dirty, that our female bodies would betray us, and that girls were the ones who had to hold the line against boys, who were basically grunting, thrusting, rabid beasts, their brains having drifted to their nether regions in the tragic aftermath of puberty. The nuns patrolled the classrooms and the schoolyard, a holy bomb squad sniffing out pheromones, nerved up and crazed from the ever-present vapor of adolescent urges fouling the very air they breathed. One day in eighth grade, a nun accused my friend of padding her bra and dragged her into the girls' room after calling in an accomplice sister from the other eighth-grade class. The nuns tag team strip-searched her, only to find that, like the woman in the classic *Seinfeld* episode, my schoolmate's breasts were real and they were spectacular. My friend escaped to public school shortly after that where she could spend the remainder of her adolescence unmolested, except by various panting boys. The rest of us learned the lesson: girls with big tits were de facto sluts. I remained under the breast radar, both grateful and resentful.

A few years ago I was at the Duomo in Milan, touring the massive cathedral built over the course of three centuries. Many of the female saints extolled to me during my days at parochial school were there in statuary, an entire football field of mutilated women. There was Saint Agatha, holding her breasts before her on a plate, as if she were waitressing at a particularly gruesome horror movie version of Hooters. Saint Agatha had them removed by pincers, in addition to being rolled over hot coals, all to preserve her virginity. Further along was Saint Lucia, her eyeballs rolling around on another plate. She plucked out her eyes and handed them to a lascivious pagan suitor who admired them, as the story went. I couldn't find Saint Catherine, but I knew her story. She had a spiked wheel named after her because she was mounted on one and revolved as knives were supposed to eviscerate her. Saint Catherine was miraculously healed after the wheel, but eventually beheaded by her disappointed pagan suitor. It made me think of all the other maimed and butchered women who had fended off the advances of men and as a result met with a hideous fate. Saint Maria Goretti, a little farm girl from southern Italy and the youngest canonized saint, was stabbed fourteen times rather than surrender her virginity.

This is just a partial list of the female role models put forward by my teachers in the eighth grade at Our Lady Help of Christians School. I was a fast learner and I got the message: death before dishonor, and sex meant dishonor.

But that's not the message I got from Ma.

Ma was at home in her body. Her sensuality was a mockery of the dire warnings my teachers gave me about hiding what was shameful and the source of sin—my prepubescent, as yet unbudded body. There she is, my mother, memory-imprinted, standing in a white rayon slip before a mirror, expertly slathering Revlon Fire and Ice on her lush lips for a mid-week night out with my father, her cleavage brimming, flaunting herself like a juicy peach waiting to be plucked. Or look at this black-and-white picture of Ma, shy but sexy, posing on a beach for my father away at war in her two-piece bathing suit, her hair a riot of black curls, arching her back just enough to thrust her breasts upward, a carnal offering to the gods of lust. No chance of those babies ending up sacrificed on a plate.

At school, the nuns wanted us to become "little Marys": ephemeral, pure, born without original sin, so feathery and not-of-this-world that we could be "assumed" into heaven, body and soul, as all the pictures celebrating the feast of the assumption showed. Mary hovered, dressed in sky blue, eyes rolled upwards toward her eventual destination as she floated above the earth, surrounded by cherubim and roses. Up, up, up she floats, her body too pure to remain on terra firma. All of us were instructed to somehow make our flawed bodies too pure for this earthly realm.

Ma was of the earth, vulgar, grounded, nasty. She horrified me: surprising me in doorways, flashing her privates with her accomplice, Aunt Ellie, my screams of mortification gratifying and turning them into mean little gigglegirls. Ma called me "Miss Prim," a perfectly apt description of myself at age twelve. Ma would never float up to heaven or anywhere else. Her coarseness revolted me so much I felt stained by her touch, and she sensed it, using my squeamishness as her secret weapon in the mother-daughter wars that flickered and flared throughout my teenage years.

As I got older, I managed to mind-mesh the floaty otherworldliness of the Blessed Virgin, the martyr horror stories of the nuns and my newfound desire for boys into an obsession with romantic and tragic love, complete with mournful Child Ballads that I memorized and droned in my room along with Joan Baez on my cheap phonograph. All of this was incomprehensible to my mother. Life was hard enough without asking for tragedy. To my mother I was Miss Prim, no better than the nuns, pitiful women who chose God for a husband.

But I secretly desired boys. Not the stammering, pimply, self-conscious nonreaders in my classes at school. I dreamed of dashing, troubled Heathcliffs galloping down my working-class street and whisking me away to some gloomy, barren landscape where we could brood together over Keatsian odes and then make turgid, doomed love. Perversely, I also dreamt of laconic cowboys, so exotic in their diffidence and calm demeanor, so different from my loud, clamorous family. It didn't matter. I was invisible to boys because I looked ten years old and had a mouth filled with flashing steel. The day I was fitted for braces was the day my social life ended. I was the only person in the whole school with braces. I was thirteen, short, underweight, flat-chested, spindly-legged, disaster-permed and haircutted, and my face was growing around my nose. It would be years before I lost the habit of covering my mouth like a geisha on the rare occasions when I laughed. But I wasn't being coy or flirtatious. I was trying to disappear myself and my steampunk mouth before someone taunted me. Inevitably, they did. The boy I worshipped from afar, whose snub nose was so small it was more of a suggestion than a breathing tube, called me "tinsel teeth." I retreated to my room and escaped into the gothic landscape once again.

All my friends were much more adept at figuring out the boy landscape with actual boys. I was good at Latin and could translate thirty lines a night. My friends were good at deciphering boys. They all wanted to remain virgins so they could have white weddings. The alternative, too terrible to ponder, was that they would be sent to a home for unwed mothers. This had happened to no one any of us knew in recent memory, but the scenario was dire enough to loom over all our high school interactions, from the most basic flirtation to the inevitable dry humping in the back seats of junkmobiles. There was no birth control available beyond "safes," and we didn't know how to get them anyway. The drugstore? We could never, ever bring ourselves to say that word to old man Fox, who knew every one of our parents, not in a million lifetimes. We didn't know they were called "condoms." We knew nothing. There was no sex education at Our Lady Help of Christians Parochial School.

We did get to see a film about sex at the girls-only retreat we attended a few weeks before we graduated. At the retreat, the sex-instruction film was creepily screened by priests, after a presentation of Fellini's *La Strada* that left most of my classmates wondering what it was supposed to be about but made me feel like I had to become an actress like Giulietta Masina, who projected an inner light so true and so luminous that she replaced the Blessed Virgin Mary's iconography in my brain the minute her face appeared on screen. *La Strada* was supposed to have some kind of religious relevance, and the Catholic Church actually funded some of the film. Giulietta Masina plays a simple-minded girl brutalized by Anthony Quinn, who buys her from her impoverished mother and puts her to work as his assistant in a moth-eaten traveling circus. She dies in the end and Anthony Quinn regrets being a beast. I got the general Catholic idea about "it's good to be a martyr because you might inspire some violent man to finally see the light and then you will have sacrificed your wretched life for something, if you can't be a breeder." This theme was reinforced by the main feature, an "educational" cartoon showing armies of sperm advancing on a huge, quivering, defenseless ovum. The film then went from animation to live action, dreamy Vaseline-lensed shots of a pregnant woman bouncing through a meadow in slo-mo, fulfilling her ultimate life purpose as a baby vessel.

At the retreat, there was another mandatory and terrifying activity following the film: face-to-face confession. The church was having a Kumbaya moment after the ecumenical council of the early sixties, and the priests were now facing us at Mass and speaking English, thus ruining any chance of letting the Latin put me into a trance state, the method that usually got me through that Sunday obligation. The Mass in English sounded stiff and somehow embarrassing and wrong, like a foreigner trying to make an elaborate pun on words she didn't understand. Now confession was required before our release back into the world and I was trapped. Why I felt I had to tell the truth during this ordeal is a mystery that haunts me even today. What I remember of the confession was the priest saying, "The boy touched you where?" and, "You must promise to never do this again or I can't grant you absolution." I solemnly promised to never do it again, and never again went to confession. I let the boy touch me again, though, because I was in love. Cloistered in my room I wrote damp, secret poetry about "chalices of flesh."

The boy about whom I confessed to the priest was my heart's delight. I may have been actually bragging, not confessing, when I described our love life to the priest. I loved the boy madly because he was The Other. He was Protestant. He was exotic, beyond my wildest dreams: he had a Chinese grandfather and almond eyes. He had a limp, from a tragic, royal disease—hemophilia. He had long black hair curling over his perfect ears and a lip that naturally curved into a sneer. I hid him from my family as long as possible, but he visited my house once, a mistake. He was curious, so I allowed him to come over. My family acted like crazed medieval townspeople circling a heretic. They didn't address him directly. Ma spoke low, guttural Italian phrases in his presence, muttering to my aunt Ellie, her eyes radiating disgust, rating my true love just below pervert on her man roster. My uncles, watching television, ignored him. My boyfriend seemed amused and unoffended, sealing our eternal love. I spirited him away before Ma tied him to a stake or cast an irreversible spell.

Ma was not surprised that I brought home a weirdo. It was the way I dressed, like a *scimmita*, like a *zingara*, like a *disgraziata*. I never asked her for the definitions of the words she spat at me. I understood the basic meaning: the only boys that would respond to my uniform of black turtleneck, sloppy jeans, and man boots were degenerates. She didn't know the English word for "degenerate," but even a *mezzo-mort'* like myself, a girl wandering the world half-dead, understood that underlying Ma's disgust was actual fear for me, fear that I would be forever alone, a *pazza*, an oddball woman who didn't know how to be a woman.

I wanted to be my own woman, and in the late sixties, that definition was changing. I didn't see my mother's earthy sensuality; what I perceived was a slave girl eternally, ridiculously deferential to men. I remembered her running my father's bath; I had a mental picture of her serving him Sunday dinner, a blank look on her face while my father gnawed a chicken leg in the background like a caveman. I remembered her telling me about her timidity on their honeymoon, about her virginal shyness. I wanted to be different from her. I wanted to be the sun, not the moon. If there was a man, I wanted him to orbit around me.

I moved into the city after graduating from Our Lady Help of Christians, into that rundown apartment on the wrong side of Beacon Hill I shared with two friends. In my mouse-hole back bedroom I had a mattress on the floor and a view of my unknown neighbor's transom. My objective, besides going to a secular college, was to lose my virginity, now that I was out in the world. The exotic hemophiliac had broken my heart. I chose a local pot dealer cold-bloodedly to be the first because he was an "older man." I realize now that means he was about twenty-five. I was eighteen. During sex I didn't know what to do; I didn't climax, like I had so many times before from just a clothes-on body-splice with my high school boyfriend and the exotic heartbreaker. The older "man" told me to move, with irritation, and I realized I was doing it wrong. I was relieved and happy when it was over and I was no longer a virgin. The next day I asked a friend if I could have one of her birth control pills and she gently explained to me how they worked. I stood in the narrow bathroom with the sickly pink walls and the eye collage over the toilet. I stared at myself in the mirror. Ma said that after you have sex, you look different forever. I wondered if I looked different now, and if so, how.

In my twenties I hate-fucked a lot of men to gain power and to exact revenge from the boys who walked away from me in high school. It worked, but the price for that first rush of power was too high and it left marks. Some of the hate that liberated me in those first years of freedom bounced back and made me hate myself. The lesson was that revenge is a dish you should leave alone, and that owner- ship of your own body is hard-won. First, you must redeem it from the church fathers who want to own it, then from the expectations and privileges of men raised in the patriarchy who want to define you by it, and then from your own complicity with the people try- ing to turn you into someone else. It was art that transformed me in the end; it was that power, not hate-fucking, that allowed me to transition and become a person who was finally myself.

When I married Chris, years after my mother had given up all hope of me ever finding someone blinkered enough to accept my unwomanly ways, my sloppy dress, my off-putting lippiness, she still couldn't believe it. I had never evolved into her image of a real woman, someone who worked her physical assets, and a man mar- ried me anyway. A handsome man, who, more wondrous to behold, was a working actor already getting awards and recognition. It wasn't about replicating Ma's relationship with my father. I perceived the electricity that crackled between them. I read, sneakily, his yearning war letters to her. I understood even before I knew consciously why we kids weren't allowed to tumble into their bed uninvited, like the innocent American kids in the sitcoms I watched. Their parents were wearing pajamas. My husband and I were different, but we had the same electricity. Ma couldn't see it. Worry about my failings as a woman clouded her judgment about us.

My mother fell so hard for my husband my sister referred mockingly to him as Saint Christopher, but she still remained perplexed if not downright suspicious about what he saw in me. She even asked him that one morning, after I sat down with my own coffee without pouring him a cup first. "How can you stand her?" My husband just laughed, further tweaking Ma's suspicions.

How could she know we were bonded by laughter and acting and sex and food? That he twanged a familiar cowboy chord from my first, dewy dreams about love? Ma probably thought I had bewitched him somehow. My husband and I joke now about *"sangue di donna,"* a love charm I read about in a book of Italian folklore. Women used their menstrual blood in a dish they cooked for the man they wanted to fall in love with them. The night we first met to run lines at my apartment I cooked him a nervous dinner of *pasta alla vongole*, running out three times for things I forgot: parsley, garlic, a bottle opener. The *fattura* was unnecessary: for a man born in Kansas City and raised on bread-and-butter sandwiches and processed cheese, the clam sauce became the spell. It was the Midwest that delivered him to me on a platter.

Despite her own gifts in that arena, Ma was wary of Chris's skill as an actor: how could we tell when he was the real Chris? Early in his career he did a heavy-breathing movie of the week where he played a domestic abuser and secret homosexual drug user. It became Ma's favorite movie, the one she sat the grandkids down to watch every time it was on. (My six-year-old nephew required a parent-teacher conference at school after bringing a clipping from *TV Guide* for show-and-tell and announcing that his uncle beat up women and did drugs.) Ma liked the operatic themes of lust and violence, but she was also known to mutter darkly: "Maybe there's a side to Chris we don' know."

"I think she's lettin' herself go." This became Ma's number-one worry after we had our son, the gnawing fear I would "let myself go" and, according to every melodrama she had ever seen on television and in the movies, Chris would as a result leave me, bedazzled by "some beautiful actress" who didn't dress in leggings and a tattered T-shirt. Ma was especially disgusted by the oversized, billowy sundresses I wore in summer. On one visit to the seaside cottage she rented every year, my husband and I were able to go on a date while my mother babysat. I wore a black, form-fitting dress and my mother was delighted. "You look-eh nice, like a prostitute," she said approvingly. The culture gap between us had never yawned wider. I wondered if she was talking tough, or being ironic, or if she actually didn't understand the meaning of the word "prostitute." Or maybe it was simply this she was saying: stop hiding your body in oversized nun clothes.

When I belatedly studied Italian a few years ago, I learned about the expression *"bella figura."* It means to make a good impression, to take pride in your appearance. The worst thing you can do in Italian society is to cut a *"brutta figura,"* an ugly representation of yourself. Weirdly, I never heard my mother use either of these terms. Perhaps she was just exhausted at seeing the sour look on my face that her Italian always evoked during my teen years. Maybe the concept seemed beyond explaining to someone proudly trailing the hems of her ragged jeans in street dirt. Years later, vacationing in my mother's hometown, my husband and I saw the *passeggiata* on Sunday, the strolling parade of well-dressed people showing off their impeccable taste in clothes. Some tiny puzzle piece about my mother clicked into place. *Bella figura.*

Was it only about the clothes? It was about so much more, about body image and approval and the ever-popular "I'm not *you*" theme that ran through our mother-daughter relationship like a tired wah-wah joke. It was undeniable that a sweep of my wardrobe then and now would reveal a closet full of clothes no different in color or style than a postulant entering the sisters of Saint Joseph mother house in 1965 would pack in her suitcase. But even though I had appropriated the all-black wardrobe of the Sisters of Saint Joseph and however much I enjoy slopping around the house in my ankle-length dresses that would be equally at home on a fundamentalist compound, I never, ever bought into their sad anhedonic cult. I love sex and my aging, scarred, well-used body. I'm not Miss Prim or a Little Mary. I'm my mother's daughter, and sometimes, when I feel like it, I even dress nice, like a prostitute.

The Hairdo Wars

"You look like-a zingara!" my mother yelled. She was calling me a Gypsy because of my wild hair.

"You look like a country-western singer," I sniped back, calling attention to the lofty architectural do my mother was sporting.

My mother and I hated each other's hair from the beginning. Not the actual hair, just the way it looked. After all, we shared the same thick, wavy manes, hers black, mine chestnut. My aunt Ellie pops in and out of this mother-daughter hair saga, too. I inherited her chestnut shade. She may have even been a more active participant in creating the many unflattering hairdos that dotted the timeline of my childhood. She was definitely responsible for the guillotine-slanted bangs that resulted whenever she got near my forehead with a pair of scissors. Ma was to blame for the banana curls hanging limply from my seven-year-old head, tortured out one springy loop at a time. The banana-curl look is particularly hideous on a long face, and while I would lose a long-face contest with Abe Lincoln, I could hold my own with, say, a cartoon Shetland pony. This strangely mid-nineteenth century look of bunched banana curls was immortalized in my second-grade school picture. When I moved to New York and wandered into the Diamond District I had uncomfortable flashbacks looking at the Hasidic men working there. I can't say it was a good look on them either, but I understand they are commanded by a higher power than their mothers to wear the face-framing tendrils and they only wear two, not an entire Medusa-like headful.

My first-grade school picture presented a raggedy-toothed underweight child with slanted bangs and a horribly-gone-wrong Tonette perm. During the at-home procedure presided over by Ma and Aunt Ellie, the too-tight pink curlers pulled at my scalp, which was already smarting from whatever disturbing chemicals were saturating my hair. My throat closed in a futile attempt to fend off the ammonia fumes. "You gotta suffer to be beautiful," Aunt Ellie said breezily, taking a deep drag of her Benson & Hedges as she handed me a tissue for my watering eyes. At school, I smiled widely for the camera, innocent, hopeful, believing utterly all the "*faccia bellas*" thrown my way by adoring relatives who pinched my cheeks and fawned over me. The day the school pictures arrived was my wake-up call, and there are no smiling school pictures of me after first grade. There followed a parade of grisly hairdos, all pasted neatly by year into Aunt Ellie's photo album.

In middle school there had been the devastating "pixie" cut, urged on by Aunt Ellie, who pushed her supposed American knowledge of the zeitgeist to override Ma in hairdo decisions. When you are in the developmental stage where your face is growing around your nose, getting a style that emphasizes and enlarges your features might not be the best idea ever. My sister, who shares my features, also lived through the mandatory pixie cut. She describes her haircut day even many years later in the same shaky PTSD terms as people who've found themselves in the direct path of killer tornados.

The unfortunate cotton-candy hair look of the early sixties required too much maintenance for it to be a success for me. Although I had enough hair to create a rat's nest of epic proportions, I had neither the skill nor the sustained interest to figure out the use of hair tools. The giant shellacked look migrated to the grownups' side of the room and my mother embraced it, or a form of it, until the day she died. The bubble cut is the first time I remember being actively horrified by Ma's hair.

The mutual dissatisfaction and back-and-forth criticism about hair continued unabated among my mother, Aunt Ellie, and me into my teens and early adulthood. As a teenager hopelessly besotted with Joan Baez and Child Ballads, I wore my hair long and unkempt, even dyeing it black to be like Joan. I pictured myself running over the moors, but instead emanated a pre-Goth girl, severely anemic look that appalled my family and made boys who'd seen too many Dracula movies afraid to come near me. Still, I was happy to have arrived at last in hairdo heaven with a style that was simply wash-and-wear. And later, when I switched to hero-worshipping Janis Joplin, my wild hair was exactly like hers, perfect for whipping around in my room during my lonely, epic lip-syncs of "Piece of My Heart."

Shortly after my move to New York City in the seventies there are resume pictures of me in what looks like a Three Stooges–type bowl cut. I have no explanation for this. There was a lull in the hairstyle battles at that time, mostly due to distance and exhaustion on both sides of the warring parties. Ma and Ellie approved of the bowl cut, and I was resigned to seeing the two of them with baroquely teased hair. I chalk up the bowl cut forever immortalized in my first acting head shots to my impulsive haircut disorder that is, thankfully, for the most part restricted to hair alone.

The impulsive haircut disorder was responsible for my split-second decision before a work trip to Los Angeles to weedwack my hair to the length of a blade of close-cropped grass. It had been too many years since the pixie cut and my memory was blurred. I was envisioning the wash-and-wear concept with very little basis in reality. I forgot that my hair is full of cowlicks and grows at an alarming rate, and that to maintain the quarter-inch-long look, I would have to become familiar with product, mostly some sort of stiffening goo, and, worse, start visiting the hairdresser every few weeks, thus defeating the whole wash-and-wear-and-forget-about-it paradigm. I was also sick of covering the white line that arose in the middle of my head every ten days. My hair had turned gray within a period of weeks when I was in my late thirties. This happened after my son arrived ten weeks early. My hair turning gray almost overnight was a side note in the cacophony of stress that surrounded my husband and me then. But in my early forties, and in the throes of the short-hair delusion, I decided to let it all go.

Ma and Ellie reacted strongly to the new hair. Not the cut, the refusal to dye it. They acted as if I had committed heresy against all of aging womankind. They were both still adding color every month and they were in their seventies, so what was I thinking? The old taunts surfaced: "Miss Prim" and "just like your aunt." Not Aunt Ellie but Auntie Sara, the one they thought of as prissy for letting her hair go gray. My husband and Jesse's caregiver, Brandy, joined the chorus. I hated to agree with them but my hair wasn't turning the pure, silky white I had seen in other, less Mediterranean types. It was more a coarse, prison-matron gray and made me look like I should be tossing cells and barking out orders at people to line up. I folded under the barrage and dyed my hair red, steeling myself for the grow-out, thankful for once that it wouldn't take long and praying that my hair would sprout like those unfurling plant tendrils in speeded-up nature films.

Ellie and Ma continued to color their hair. Ma died a blonde at the age of eighty-four. Ellie always said that my uncle Benny was the one who wanted her to keep her chestnut hair, but a few years before she died, she stopped coloring it. Even though I had teased both Ellie and Ma about dyeing their hair, I was sad when Ellie stopped that gesture toward what was once her youth.

Whenever the topic of my hair came up in later years, Aunt Ellie would sigh and tell me, "I liked when you had the shag," referring to a fleeting eighties do. "That's when your hair really looked good." "Well," I would respond with irritation, "that would be great if I wanted a frozen-in-time look like you and Ma." Ellie would laugh and I would continue, loftily: "I choose to move on."

But I haven't moved on. My hair is now blonde, the same color as my mother's. And the last time I was in New York, I had my hair cut into a shag. I think it looks good on me.

When Ma Was a Lunch Lady

Ma stood in a line of old women ladling inedible glop onto beige melamine plates and shoving them forward to the sluggish teen-agers awaiting them. She was unrecognizable, an impersonator of my mother. Her glossy black hair was bound up in an ugly hair-net and her face was wearing the glowering mask of her new self. Ma was the youngest, the prettiest in the cafeteria line; she didn't belong with those grizzled harridans. I stood waiting for the glop behind the most popular girls at my school. I was a member of that group, the popular girls, even if at times my belonging felt like an act of noblesse oblige on their part, the grudging forbearance of the court fool. I was defiant and funny in a quirky way, and that was my reason for belonging to the crowd that knew how to talk to boys. It helped that I had grown up with most of them. I was fifteen and a junior at my parochial school. I wore the Our Lady Help of Chris-tians school uniform: a stiff powder-blue vest, the color attributed to the Virgin Mary; a navy-blue skirt; and a white blouse with a Pe-ter Pan collar and short sleeves. It was attractive on no one and this was the intent. I watched my mother, the interloper, move without grace. I wished I were dead. I wished Ma had died instead of my father, because my father would never humiliate me by becoming a cafeteria worker in my own school if Ma had been the one who died. He would have just gone behind his bar and we would have all been fine, just fine. I never fantasized how I would've run the household at age fifteen, since immigrant-family tradition would expect that of me, the oldest girl; I couldn't cook, run the washer, iron clothes, or shop for food. I only knew how to lose myself in books and listlessly wiggle a dust mop across the floor after Ma yelled so loud I couldn't concentrate on *Wuthering Heights* or *Forever Amber.*

The nuns patrolled the sickly-green-colored lunchroom, keeping order amid the miasma of bad smells emanating from the ersatz food, demanding absolute quiet as if we teenagers were the ones who had taken vows of silence and become members of their self-denying cult. Girls sat with girls and boys with boys. We stood on separate sides from one another at recess, where we were forbidden to cross the great divide. It was only on Friday nights, at the Catholic Youth Organization dances, that we were expected to magically discover the ability to socialize without awkwardness, to embrace each other in virtuous dances overseen by priests. The priests refused admittance to any sluts who dared entrance to the dance with a pullover sweater outlining their budding breasts, instead of a cardigan decently buttoned over a blouse. I was a wallflower at the Friday-night dances; I read too many books and actually tried to engage teenage boys in discussions about these books, proving my own disengagement with reality. Usually the boys just muttered, "You're weird," before turning away, their faces crooked with contempt.

Not long after my father died, a priest got my mother that job at my school as a lunch lady. She must have been desperate to let the parish priest get her a job, given her withering contempt of all things clerical. In her life before my father's death, she was an anticleric, a real *mangiaprete,* literal translation: priest-eater. But she couldn't drive a car. She could barely read or write in English.

She had three kids and inherited a business she couldn't run: my father's bar, smoky and belonging to the realm of men only, men with loud voices barking out drink orders, yipping with laughter at dirty jokes, or snarling at each other in drunken furies that spilled over into fistfights. She didn't belong there. She sold the bar at a loss, one more dream to meet a mortal end that year. Ma must have felt like she didn't belong anywhere after my father died. Neither did I, but we were each on distant planets of pain, never even in the same orbit, the same galaxy, the same universe.

My brother, wandering lost in his own desolate eighth-grade wasteland, was happy to see my mother at school, happy at the extra portions of the inedible American glop ladled onto his plate, becalmed by any signs of love awakened from his dark-with-grief mother. He didn't feel, as I did, a keen sense of agony at the sight of our mother dethroned from her place as queen of her own savory kitchen, in servitude now to food that was unspeakable, a sacrilege. I didn't know that was what I felt then, a grief from the loss of my father made exponential by the rippling devastation to the rest of my family. My little sister, only seven, reverted to sucking her thumb and crept, white-faced, into rooms, silent, watchful, afraid to say my father's name and thus retrigger the opera of grief that had surrounded his immediate death.

Daddy was diagnosed at fifty with esophageal cancer in August, his birthday month, and dead sixty-odd days later, at the end of October. He was at first enraged, then ashamed of the life force draining from his body, at what he saw as his failure to protect his family. One day at dinner I watched him choke on his food, then angrily throw his napkin down and stalk out of the room. I didn't understand that he was dying, not because my mother and extended family were trying to protect me from this knowledge, but because I went through those days in an impenetrable cocoon of adolescent self-regard.

Maybe that's why Ma didn't care about food anymore. After her beautifully hand-wrought meals began to choke my father, the man she loved above all others, the one who had saved her from her own mournful self, maybe she sought penance in the third circle of hell that was Our Lady's cafeteria. Maybe she somehow blamed herself for being unable to save him with her greatest superpower, the ability to create life-sustaining, soul-redemptive food with her own two hands. Maybe she felt like this was the place she belonged: in this steamy, slimy, faux-spaghetti abyss, mocked by overcooked pasta soaked in ketchup with cubes of pencil-eraser-like American cheese on the side.

No one teased me because Ma was a lunch lady. All my friends were lower middle class, like me. A lot of them already had jobs after school. Even I, the most hopelessly irresponsible member of the group, had taken a one-day-a-week job babysitting for a rich family's overactive kid on the other side of town. Still, I felt ashamed for Ma, for the way she had fallen in the world. It wasn't the menial nature of her job; it was the fact that she was alone now, and without status in her paired-off social circle. I remembered how Ma had told me, with a touch of smugness, how Daddy always made sure to dance with the widows when they went to a wedding, so they wouldn't feel alone. In her former couples-only social scene, she herself would now be an outcast, the widow in black who sat alone at weddings.

Ma wore black from head to toe after my father died. She never intended to take it off. Where she came from, you honored your dead by removing color from your life, just as their presence had drained the world around you of anything bright. We all objected: her baffled kids, her American-born sisters-in-law, her friends. You're in America, now, they said. We don't do that here. Your husband wouldn't want that. Only old ladies dress like that. You're young. You need to live your life, they said. Ma said nothing, acting as if she didn't hear.

But little by little, Ma began to live her life. She began by leaving behind the lunchroom at Our Lady's within the year, so that by the time I was a senior she was gone, to my great relief. At her future job, she would cook the kind of food that made her happy, for outlaws from her country who would appreciate dishes that reminded them of home. And, using her other skill, juggling numbers, she would also become a part-time bookie, calling in her three-digit lists to the local wise guy, a job she kept until the end of her life, a life now lived with the pale, seeping return of color and a bittersweet, cautious joy somehow taking root in a bedrock of sorrow.

My friend Dorothy and I have an e-mail contest over who had the best resting bitch face as a teenager. I win when I find a photograph of the day of my graduation party from Our Lady's. I am standing, flanked by my mother, my aunt Ellie, and Tiny, a family friend. They are smiling with good cheer and dressed up for my special day. I am holding a knife. I stare directly into the camera without expression, like a serial killer. I hope I look like a serial killer when the photograph is taken. I am about to cut into my graduation cake, a white frothy concoction from Antoine's bakery. I am the first person to graduate from high school in the history of my family, a long line of Italian peasants from the mountains of the *meridionale*. I am terrified for the future and furious with everyone in my family for denying my self-recognized genius. I am also enraged at my father, for being dead. I want to go to college. I have vague dreams of being a journalist, like Nellie Bly. But the nuns won't give me a recommendation for a non-Catholic college. I can't afford a Catholic college. I don't know how to go to college, any college. My family wants me to go to secretarial school and marry someone from the neighborhood. If I can't figure out how to go to college I might have to do what they want. This makes me surly and closed. So why are they so happy at my graduation? They think this is the apex of what I can achieve. They are satisfied for me, think I should be satisfied, too. I repudiate my smiling mother, my grinning aunt, and stand there, expressionless. I will not join in their celebration.

I will play by their rules, go to secretarial school for two weeks, drop out, get a job, save up for an apartment, move out, and go to a state school I can afford. Ma and I trade faces then, and I am finally smiling while she wears the carefully crafted mask of rage.

After the tearful scenes, the doleful head-shakings, the dire predictions, the scowls of disapproval from my close and extended family, I move into my first apartment, the three-room dump that I share with two equally unworldly friends. Together, we reach a breathless level of incompetence and irresponsibility fueled by drugs and the mad exhilaration of freedom from adult supervision. I am barely eighteen. I do not know how to pay utilities or what to do if the refrigerator breaks. I don't know how to shop for groceries or operate a washing machine.

A few months after the move, my mother tells me she wants to see the apartment. I am happy at what I view as her concession. Ma agrees to meet me in town, which is how we always referred to going into Boston. She doesn't commandeer the slavish, perennially doomed-to-failure suitor who drives her on errands. Instead, she takes public transportation, something I doubt she's done since her earliest days as an immigrant working in the Garment District. We meet at Park Street station. I see that she is dressed in a suit, as if she were meeting with officials, but I think it is more in tribute to the fact that she is "in town." I am wearing bell-bottom jeans, the hems of which trail in the street. Ma doesn't mention my outfit. We have lunch at a nearby place that serves clam-plate dinners for ninety-nine cents. We are formal and silent during our lunch. I cannot remember a time when I have ever eaten alone with my mother in a restaurant.

We walk across Boston Common to Beacon Hill and climb the two flights to my apartment. I dig out my key with pride and open the door. I try not to see the three small rooms through my mother's eyes: the curtainless, dirty windows; the pillows on the floor that serve as seating; the tiny kitchen with room only for one person at a time to stand comfortably and open the refrigerator. I don't open the refrigerator because it is empty and I don't want to hear my mother sigh. Besides my job at the Tarry 'n' Taste donut shop, I am waitressing at a folk music club. I'm going to Andy Warhol films, ice-skating stoned on the Frog Pond in the Boston Common, and committing civil disobedience at protests against the Vietnam War. I feel exultant and free doing this, like a girl in a foreign film.

My mother doesn't see the newly liberated me. She sees the wobbly table in the corner, the rickety chairs, the incomprehensible "Russell killed an ounce on this spot" scrawled on the wall. She uses the bathroom and looks at the eye collage near the toilet, left there by some meth freaks, previous tenants. She views my tiny room, the mattress on the floor, the candle beside the bed. She stifles her moan, but her eyes are damp. She is no doubt thinking of my room at home with the apple tree just outside the window, the pink wallpaper, the frilly coverlet, the orphaned dolls huddled against the flowery pillow.

I wished then that my mother could remember herself at eighteen. I wanted Ma to recall her own desperate bid for freedom, the need above all else to become her own self that made her say good-bye to the place she knew best, to the mother she loved. But when I brought it up in a clumsy attempt to show a parallel between us, she rewrote her history. Now she hadn't wanted to leave at all. It was circumstances, others, her father, the threat of forced marriage, the war—she would never have left her mother for something as selfish as a vague desire to be free. I had heard all this revisionist history before, in the operatic scenes that precluded my move, but we said nothing now as I walked Ma to the Charles Street station at the end of her visit. We said good-bye and I turned and walked up the steep slope of Anderson Street, back to my own apartment where I was both unhappy and free.

Ma and the Mob

"I 'ad dinner with a jewelah," Ma said.

Or that's what it sounded like. I took my cues off Ma's demeanor, since her Italian-Boston accent seemed particularly impenetrable that day. Or maybe it was because I was now living in Manhattan surrounded by that unique medley of voices, and the sounds of home were becoming dim. It was my goal as a future working actor to subdue those sounds that marked me as a Boston native. Now, on this visit home, I felt the carefully honed regionalisms I had worked so hard to eradicate seeping back into my speech. Fifteen minutes after I stepped off the bus, I was already dropping *r*'s like a Kennedy.

Ma seemed somehow proud of her dinner announcement. She had a smile curling at the corner of her mouth and a self-satisfied air as she stood at the stove frying eggplant, turning occasionally to place a finished one on a plate near my sister, Lindy, and me. We sat around the kitchen table like baby birds, mouths open, waiting for food. The kitchen, as always, acted as a time tunnel and transformed us into helpless toddlers in the face of our mother's culinary expertise. I wondered if her dinner with the jeweler meant that Ma had decided to start seeing men. My father had been dead for a number of years. All three of us kids wanted Ma to date, although we couldn't actually picture our mother with another man.

"That's nice," I responded, uncertain as someone picking their way through a snaky bog. "Are you going on dates with a jeweler now?" My mother barked her non-laugh laugh. She looked as if she pitied me for my cluelessness. This was a familiar expression. I sent a distress signal to my sister, Lindy, the downward mouth-pull that was our code, designed to be imperceptible to our mother. One of us often acted as translator to the other when Ma's responses seemed stranger than usual.

"She means Angiulo," my sister said flatly, as if she were asking me to hand her a dishtowel. Now my mother was happy, noting my puzzled response. "Yeah, nice guy," she added. "Isn't he, uh, connected to the mob?" I asked. It was pretty common knowledge in the 1970s that the Angiulo brothers, from Boston's North End, were made men in the Patriarca crime family. My mother shook her head, disgusted. "'E's a nice guy," she said again, her tone challenging this time. I dropped it before the sound of her voice descended any lower and the threat level rose higher. She slammed another fried eggplant slice on the plate and I speared it greedily before my sister got to it.

Ma was happy at her new job, cooking at an Italian restaurant just up the street from our house, near my father's old bar. Leone's Café was long gone, now a travel agency. Ma preferred being surrounded by wise guys to the lunch ladies at my old high school. At the new place, she was praised lavishly for dishes that evoked grandma memories in its hard-guy patrons. They swooned and kissed her reverently when my mother delivered a replica of a beloved nonna's macaroni and Sunday gravy. My mother, alone too long, basked in the glow of attention from young men, even if they were only offering the sexless devotion of pilgrims at a family shrine. She was in her late forties, her big brown eyes dimmed by sorrow but her presence still vivacious, her ripe figure still turning heads.

I visited Ma's new restaurant on Talent Night. There was live music but the place was still empty and the Frank Sinatra impersonations had not yet begun. I arrived near the end of Ma's shift and waited for her in the bar. This area of the restaurant was as dark and smoky as my father's working-class, all-male bar, but here there were aspirations to a classier, mixed clientele, as evidenced by the glossy dark-wood tables, porn-glow lighting, and the ruby-red shag carpeting. There was an off-the-Vegas-Strip vibe to the place, but the only hints of gambling activity were the whispered consults at the far end of the bar, as guys with Beckettian names like Gogo and Fifi took action on Sunday's games.

I sat uncomfortably at a table waiting for Ma, feeling judged. Guys like Fifi and Gogo didn't like hippie chicks like me, as a rule. They did like that we were supposed to be easy, but they didn't approve of the lack of makeup and sloppy grooming. My mother heartily agreed with the *why-os* at her place of work about my unadorned lips and stupid-looking oversized peasant tops and blue jeans with ragged, filthy hems. The irony of wearing peasant tops around my peasant mother was lost on me. I felt comfortable and groovy in them. One of the low talkers, Fifi or Gogo, materialized out of nowhere when I nervously took out a cigarette. Before I brought it to my lips, he produced a lighter with a flourish, like a troubadour offering a poem. He asked silkily if I wanted a drink, but I refused. I looked down on drinkers. I knew that the drink offer wasn't a come-on, just a reflexive courtesy because I was a girl sitting alone. To guys like Fifi I was nothing more than an oddity, like a counting chicken or a cat that could use the toilet. I was offended by this guy's appraisal, even though the idea of having a Fifi as a boyfriend was as odd to me as a cat using a toilet.

Ma waded serenely through the swamp of illegal activities, dispensing calamari rings like sacramental wafers. She must have felt like she finally belonged somewhere. The young widow, unwelcome in the world of couples, was now a favorite and a confidante to even younger men. The pitiful young widow, newly bereaved, given a charity job by the church to hand out pitiful food, was now serving her own glorious meals and valued for it. When she emerged from the kitchen of her new place, she held herself with a revived kind of bearing just short of a strut. She was more herself and less the woman who had revolved as the outer moon of my ebullient father's Jovian personality. No longer the uncertain young widow, she was at home in her new world.

Even if that new world meant finding a dead body by the trash barrels one day when she went out to dump some garbage. Ma told me that news during our weekly phone call. Her delivery was calm, almost offhand. I felt a surge of jealousy that surprised me. I was in New York City, pursuing an acting career, but all I had to report was being rejected at yet another cattle-call audition or the daily drudgery of temping at a job where my comb-over boss summoned me by snapping his fingers and my sad-sack permanent office mate's unwashed hair filled every cubic inch of air in the jail cell–sized office with the smell of stale popcorn. Ma was the one with the breaking news, not me, the person living in a world-class city. Ma also had good gossip from her job: which *assahole* guy left his wife for a twenty-four-year-old mistress who then dumped him; which jealous wife painted swear words on her cheating husband's car; who got arrested and who fell on the floor wailing at Magni's Funeral Home in front of the coffin at a long-estranged sister's wake.

What Ma left out of that conversation was her new part-time job. My sister told me Ma was booking numbers on the side and reporting directly to the Fifis and Gogos of the world. Everyone in our neighborhood played the numbers, the three-digit illegal lottery based on the outcome of the daily horse races. Ma was enthusiastic about playing three-digit street addresses of note, birthdays, and, highest in priority, numbers given by deceased relatives in dream messages. Even though she had never read a book in her life, she was facile with numbers. And she had a memory that was prodigious. I could testify firsthand to her ability to re-call a slight, some going all the way back to her girlhood village in Abruzzi and involving long-dead perpetrators. I thought she would be a great bookie, but I also had a momentary fantasy about the middle-of-the-night phone call and having to bail out my own mother. But that was a fantasy because she was the one who bailed me out, more than once, not from jail (though I came close during the antiwar protests of the sixties) but from heartbreak, depres-sion, and fear, even though she had her own woes. Ma wasn't up-beat or Pollyanna-ish in the least. In fact, she was always so eager to go to the dark side that I would inevitably, perversely start to feel upbeat about the situation that had originally depressed me. For example, I would tell her about some audition I had lost and mourn about how I would probably never get to be an actress, and she would agree, telling me it was "too hard" and that I should come home. I would then be predictably outraged and fire off all the reasons that I would succeed in becoming a working actress and accuse her of trying to kill my life's dream. It worked every time, as if we were characters in some absurdist play following the same script that took place in the same mother-daughter limbo setting in a no-time zone.

Ma never got arrested. Instead, she made the Wall of Fame at the local luncheonette up the street from where she lived most of her life in our close-knit neighborhood. I took my elderly aunt for a quick bite not long ago after a doctor's visit that seems to be the main reason for an outing when you're in your nineties. There she was, Ma in her later years, her blonde hair a dandelion puffball, surrounded by connected guys. She was the only woman on the wall, the Mystery Grandma, High Priestess of Numbers, and the Mona Lisa smile she flashed was one I had never seen anywhere else.

And when I came across one of her little green notebooks years after her death, migrated somehow into my own messy desk drawer, I saw her tentative but neat columns of three-digit numbers, and I thought of it as my very own Rosetta Stone, a code as yet unbroken.

Miltuh, or While I Was Gone

"*What, I gotta* take cayuh some ol' man now?"

This was Ma's stock response to anyone asking if she ever thought about marrying again. But when the restaurant where she cooked for the wise guys of the Lake burned down, she was out of a job, except for booking numbers on the side. She found another one, right across the street from our house. The factory that had been there for years was long gone, and the buildings were now part of an office park. There was a restaurant mainly frequented by the office staff run by a mild, sweet man named Milton, a man who bore not the slightest resemblance to our Sun God father. Milton was not very tall, soft-spoken, about eight years younger than Ma, and quietly delighted by everything about her. He was also Jewish, which mattered to no one in our Catholic-in-name-only family except one distant great-aunt by marriage, and no one paid any attention to her squawks of manufactured outrage.

Years had passed since our father's death. Ma was in her early fifties now, and my brother and sister and I didn't want her to be alone. For selfish reasons on my part, I wished Ma had something better to tell me during her mournful, somehow accusatory weekly phone calls complaining about my little sister, my younger brother, the bleakness of her life. My mother and I had effectively abandoned each other during this time. I was distracted and distant when we spoke, only expressing my real feelings in my journal, a rant-filled exercise in self-absorption that was so relentless I even disgusted myself, signing off as "stoned and raving" . . . until the next raving mememe entry.

When Ma and Milton became an item, everything changed. There had been no men in her life for years, except for one seriously short guy with the literal name of a clown who hung around like a lingering cough. He was a leftover from the days when my father would send guys from the bar to our house to drive my mother wherever she needed to go, since she never got her driver's license. After my father died, this clown-named man still drove her places and used to hug her hopelessly and tell her he loved her, after which Ma would swat him away like a fly. He was child-sized and the gesture must have been reflexive on Ma's part. My friends and I snickered over the fact that he had a little plate with "This car belongs to" and his real name engraved on a shiny, gold business-card-sized sign screwed into the dashboard of his boat-like seventies car. In the back of the car were bobbleheads, lined up. We jeered at that, too. But I also took advantage of his generous nature by cadging rides from him whenever I needed them on the rare occasions when I visited home. I looked down on my mother's dependency on others to drive her around, but I didn't get my own driver's license until years later.

I was living in Boston, having deserted Beacon Hill to share a roomy but run-down apartment in a triple-decker house in Mission Hill, on the edge of Roxbury. I rode my bike to school at UMass-Boston from my apartment that had a pantry and a huge kitchen and a falling-down back porch. It was also a magnet for robbers, and we were broken into at least three times while my roommate and I lived there. Our Norman Batesian landlord informed us of his creepy plan to smear his home-made napalm on the back doorknobs as a deterrent to future robbers. We put up with him because the rent was dirt cheap. I was consumed with finishing school (after dropping out twice) and getting a job so that I could move to New York City and begin my life as an actress. I never went home any more. It was as if my family were a group of people I vaguely recalled from a boring party I had once attended that had gone on forever and now was glad to have finally escaped.

Does this all sound really mean? It's because I'm slipping back into an extremely mean, narcissistic period in my life and now it's seeping into this story. Just know that I'm not this mean now. Although it's scary how easily I can call it up, this meanness.

Ma was going out every Saturday night with Milton, my little sister reported. They went to New York to see *Hair* on Broadway. This Ma told me herself when I went home for Thanksgiving. She giggled about the nude cast onstage and about seeing New York again after so many years. As Ma's elation grew, so did her hair, until her hairstyle reached the giddy heights of a lady-in-waiting at court with Marie Antoinette. I was both relieved and uneasy over the strangeness of seeing my mother lighthearted for the first time in years. My aunts and uncles seemed happy for her. Ma bustled around the table, serving us first and sitting down only after everyone was eating, as always, but this year Milton was with us, although my uncle Benny still sat at the head of the table.

For the next ten years, Milton was a fixture. He bought my little sister her first car. He managed restaurants for a living, so he got me a job at a hamburger joint in Harvard Square, where I endured snotty Radcliffe girls asking me what was the "soup du jour." He took my mother out to dinner every weekend or to his cottage on Cape Cod. Milton classed up the joint, sitting in our living room with his Andy Williams sweaters and his low-maintenance ways. Now when I went home at Christmas, it was like opening the door and entering through some off-kilter upper-middle-class prism. All the traditional foods were being served for the night before Christmas, the feast of the seven fishes that now also included Italian sausages and pork ravioli. My mother had been replaced by someone from a '70s movie of the week, dressed in fancy heels and a long hostess gown, and her friends and, more surprisingly, the rest of my adult family were also decked out as if they were playing twenty-one at a casino in Monte Carlo. It was all good, I thought. Theirs was a middle-aged romance, tender and low-key. I liked Milton, who listened patiently to my tirades on politics and my judgments on everything (and at twenty I judged everything, always). I was happy that Ma was happy because, selfishly, I no longer needed to feel guilty about her sorrow. One Christmas Eve, Milton gave Ma a diamond ring. It all went downhill from there.

Dead for over five years, my father's ghostly self was still the spirit that dominated our house. There he was, sitting in his chair from which he roared with laughter every night at my brother's dead-on impersonation of Jackie Gleason in *The Honeymooners*. There were his books, overflowing the built-in bookcases. Outside, his grape arbor, where he sat with his friends, pouring wine suffused with peaches on a summer day. His bocce court. His stone wall that he built himself. He was everywhere. Milton wanted my mother to sell our haunted house and move with him to another once close by, a new ranch, expunged of memories of my father.

My mother couldn't sell our house. She sensed my aunt Ellie's disapproval. Aunt Ellie, who had welcomed Milton warmly, was attached to the house where she grew up, the house the family had worked hard to save during the Depression, part of the family lore retold during every holiday. The house stood for all kinds of things beyond the memories of my aunt's brother, her mother, and father. It was the American dream made manifest, our little arts and crafts house with the garage and big yard, the grape arbor, the apple and pear trees, my father's carefully tended rock garden with poppies that still bloom today. My mother felt like the house was her legacy to us, her children. She was unmoved by financial plans from Milton, plans that would leave an even greater legacy than the house, a monetary one that probably would make more sense, since all three of us would never live there together. But the idea of selling the house remained unthinkable, no matter how many times Milton brought it up. Eventually, he got tired of bringing it up.

The steady drip of Ma's numerous refusals to move to another house with Milton finally eroded their relationship. After it ended and Milton moved on, Ma was inexplicably outraged and blamed him as if he had cheated on her, thrown her over, lied to her, or any number of soap-opera scenarios that didn't actually happen. The relationship came to a standstill and then withered away because Ma wouldn't take the next step to let it move on.

Ma continued to act as though she was the injured party. She even consulted her *strega* to put a curse on Milton (eerily, it worked; his next relationship failed, plagued by a number of problems).

When some years had gone by, Ma and Milton reconciled, at least by phone. He was living in another state, and they spoke from time to time, Ma not quite able to keep the resentment out of her voice, nor the satisfaction that he had not found happiness in his life without her. My sister and her family still live in our old house, but I often wish that Ma and Milton had reconciled their differences and were able to marry or live together into mutual old age. He had slipped so easily into our family dynamic, his amiable nature allowing my mother to shine, where my father's outsized personality had cast her in his shadow, albeit an agreeable and adoring one, in her early years as wife and mother. Milton would have tempered her bitterness, surely, but never the bred-in-the-bone cynicism that was DNA-imprinted in Ma. Still, it is easy to picture them aging together, travelling with my aunt and uncle on their yearly trips to Aruba, hosting family feasts. Milton wrote to me after Ma died. I have lost the letter, but I still remember the compassion and sorrow it held. Maybe he, too, was wistful for what could have been, and maybe Ma was the love of his life. Or maybe I didn't get the cynicism gene and I'm a hopeless romantic. But it was the poet Virgil who said, *"Amor vincit omnia, et nos cedamus amori."* "Love conquers all things, so we too shall yield to love." I wish Ma had yielded to love a second time in her life.

Serial Embellisher

"Dorothea, c'mere," my mother hissed, gesturing toward the bedroom. Once inside, Ma thrust an oversized card at my friend, the word "Daughter" featured in large glittery letters on the front. She whispered with the urgency of a bomb dismantler, "You write for me. You the movie writer. My words are no good." My friend was a film producer, but the occupation was in the same ballpark from my mother's point of view: an unimaginable profession. Ma showed her a necklace with a zircon-encrusted heart dangling at its center and told Dorothy the story she wanted written on the card. My friend, charmed, wrote out the romantic scenario my mother narrated as they huddled in my son's bedroom.

Later, Ma presented me with the card and the necklace. Dorothy hovered in the background just behind her, waiting for my reaction, jiggling with excitement. I smiled back at Dorothy, taking in her innocent, credulous face, her happy expectation of the sentimental, teary scene about to unfold.

The front of the card read *"Daughter, you've given me such special memories."* It was hard to quell the Dana Carvey "special" voice that popped up in my head, but the years of actor training kicked in and I kept my smile genuine, I hoped, like a ghostly remnant of a more earnest self. I opened the card and scanned quickly its treacly message about how these special memories grow more precious every year . . . and on and on into the realm of borderline insulin shock. The card ended with a birthday wish, though it wasn't my birthday just then. Next came Dorothy's printed message outlining the story my mother had dictated to her: *"Dear Marianne, This is the first gift your father gave me the second time we met. We were in a little small restaurant in Newton. I had to pay the bill because he said 'I'm sorry . . . I don't have any money.' Then he said, 'I want you to have this because I love you and I want you to marry me.' That was sixty years ago. It's not much, but I want you to have this to remember me and your father forever. Love always,* (and here my heart cracked open, a little) *Linda Leone."*

Yes, my mother signed her full name as if the card were a legal document and I was some high-court magistrate waiting to grant her something: Love? Acceptance? Belief in her lifted from a romance-novel story? It seemed like she was groveling for favor, and I felt like an ancient Roman emperor deciding on thumbs up or down. A sudden onrush of pity for that officially signed name engulfed me like a rising tide. And, just as quickly, I resented her, outraged at her brazen and elaborate fictions, the manipulation, the need for a dramatic scene in a play I didn't want to perform.

I knew the story was bogus. The necklace was an eighties piece of costume jewelry from Kmart. Not one bit of it sounded true. My proud father invites her to dinner, then forgets to bring any money but remembers to bring a necklace and propose to her? The whole baroque fable made me squirm. But a small part of me admired her brio. So I smiled tenderly and hugged my mother. Now in her early eighties, she felt slight, her once-sensual body waning into old age. I hoped I was convincing, though I knew my mother would have liked tears. I saw the disappointment in her wounded eyes at my muted response. My own anger, hidden, smoldered and threatened to flash into life. I hugged her again, to cover up my tell-all face. I looked over her shoulder, smirking at my friend, who looked puzzled. Later, I debunked Ma's entire fantasy to Dorothy. I was ruthless and biting and funny, and my friend laughed, but we were both let down in a strange way, I, because I felt like a traitor, and my friend, because she liked the mythical story and wished it were true.

My mother was versatile in other fictional genres, her ability to rewrite history most often lending itself to the noir. The tale she told about her father's death was graphic and horrible as a war crime. My mother grew up on a farm in the Abruzzi, on a desolate stretch of land shadowed over by the Gran Sasso, the largest mountain in Italy. She claimed that her father died by falling off a barn roof onto the horns of a bull, a death that seemed both violent and cartoonishly impossible, even as she told it. Ma couldn't quite hide the satisfaction in her voice as she related the story. I gathered that she hated him from the time I had visited Italy and videotaped her half-sister talking about my grandfather. I was asking my zia Santina in my execrable Italian to tell me about "nonno." She was shy but faced the camera and said her father was *allegri* (cheerful) and had lots of friends. Back in the states, I was excited to show my mother. Standing in my living room, watching the video, Ma snorted like the bull that had supposedly gored her father. The bull, as it turned out, of her imagination. This was made clear to me when my mother's Italian half-sister, puzzled, corrected my version of her father's death and told me he died from a fall. It was off the roof, but not onto the horns of a bull. He just hit his head and died, a bare, unadorned death, the kind of farm accident that was, unfortunately, all too common in Ma's part of the world.

The writer in me can see the need for my mother to embellish her father's death, to add a twist of revenge for all the times Ma had to run for help when he was beating her mother. She was a frightened child in a lonely farmhouse listening to unholy sounds in the dark night. For Ma, the new and improved tale of her father's fall off the roof is a better, more just ending. The horns, symbol of the cuckold, were an almost unconscious elaboration from Ma, repeating the story of her mother wanting to leave her father for someone else. Ma was a genius at semiotics.

In the alternate story of my grandfather's life, the one told by Ma's stepsister, all that rage and bluster didn't exist, because my grandfather's new wife was someone who was glad to be married to him, and that made him *allegri*, the happy man described by my aunt in Italy. For my mother, it was picturing the horns and the Grand Guignol demise of her father that made her happy.

My own marriage was subject to Ma's compulsive storytelling and rewriting. The meme she continued to push despite all evidence to the contrary was that I was "starving" my husband, somehow not allowing him to eat his fill. This fantasy probably arose from the fact that Chris is lanky, with a slender frame, though he has a great appetite, especially for Italian food (not surprising for someone who grew up in the Midwest on gray overcooked vegetables and frozen food). Once, while visiting the cottage she rented every year on the Cape, she overheard me ask Chris for twenty dollars. My sister told me Ma bemoaned to her the fact that I had to "beg" my husband for spending money. Like it or not, Chris and I were stock characters in a *romanza* born of Ma's feverish imagination.

Ma was also a drama queen, sometimes preferring to act out her embellishments. But her true forte was comedy. She always tipped her hand at drama, and it was hard not to laugh at what was supposed to be a heart-wrenching or tragic scene.

Like the time my friends Rich and Nancy came back with me from New York for a visit home. I had gone upstairs for something and arrived back in the hallway just in time to hear Ma's mournful voice from the kitchen telling my friends, "You so good to be friends with Muddy-Ahn. She *need* friends. . . ." I ran into the kitchen, aghast. From her tone, I fully expected to find my mother on her knees with a shawl on her head, plucking at Rich's pant leg as she begged him and Nancy to show me a crumb of kindness, unworthy as I was of it. I wondered what alternate versions of my life were being emoted to others besides the Alone and Friendless in the Big City model.

In another encounter with my friend Dot, Ma exhibited her acting chops in the horror genre:

Ma crouched in the undergrowth by the pool. "*Pssst,*" she whisper-shouted. She beckoned to Dot, hands close to her chest, looking over her shoulder as if she were in a war zone and a sniper might pick her off from the deck above. My friend parked her car in our driveway and opened the door, no doubt wondering why my mother was cowering in front of the Rose of Sharon bush like a deranged garden gnome. "C'mee, c'mee, c'mee," my mother said, curling her fingers. When Dot got close enough, my mother shriek-whispered her news.

"She's *terrible!* Jus' watch it when you go in there. She's in a *mood.* Poor Chris! *Terrible!*"

Ma was spending the week with us that summer. I have no recollection of what I had done to Chris that was *terrible* and made my mother feel she had to be a sentinel to warn guests to beware my monstrous ways.

Ma's skills in the thriller category were, arguably, her best. After she died, one of the ladies from her weekly hair-salon group told me that Ma made a theatrical entrance one day, out of breath, as she flung open the door to Suzy's.

"Gimme a quarter! I need a quarter right away! Who's got a quarter?"

Ma was agitated and looked like someone about to report a crime. Hair dryers flew upwards, hairspray was halted, and the ozone layer was spared for another minute. The ladies, alarmed, gathered 'round my mother.

With exquisite timing, she waited until their anxious queries died down.

"I wanna call Jerry! [my father, who had been dead for at least thirty years at that time] I wanna know why he leave me and no come to me in a dream!"

I understand the allure of changing the outcome of a situation. After all, I have a direct genetic link to a serial embellisher, someone who saw no harm in making a character more interesting, ratcheting up the drama, rewriting the plot of a mundane story to something juicy, something more satisfying than the random, no-fault, disappointing scenarios that the everyday world has to offer. It's tempting to become the god of your own alternate universe.

I do it whenever I can. Only I'm not good at making up stories, like Ma. As a mostly nonfiction writer, I am doomed to my own version of the truth, as filtered through memoir or essay. But as an actor, I get to indulge in my inherited craving to become someone else, even if that person is a bitter, aggrieved alcoholic or a sweet-tempered nun (a true stretch for me) or a tough cookie with a shriveled walnut where her heart used to be. I admit to also having inherited Ma's over-emoting gene. I once worked for six months on stillness in acting class to try to control my rubbery features. Every time I step outside of my own reality and into someone else's skin, I think of my mother and her blurry relationship with truth, her desire to heighten every story, her urge to take center stage. And I watch old black-and-white Italian movies for clues: is this deep well of passion something Ma is accessing from a national gene pool?

I remember asking my mother if there were any theaters in her hometown. "We had opera," she said. "And the processions." I saw one of the processions my mother described, one that is famous in Italy, *La Madonna che scappa*, the Running Madonna, an Easter ritual that reunites the grieving mother with her transfigured Son. It takes place in my mother's town square, the Piazza Garibaldi, with six men carrying the black-draped Madonna on a bier. Dressed in green chasubles, they sway and march toward the church at the other end of the piazza, where the doors will suddenly open and the grieving mother, "seeing" her Son alive again, "runs" toward him. Her black robes fly off, doves fly out, and the Hallelujah chorus blares over the loudspeakers. There is a crowd reaction of tears, and the men who carried the Madonna embrace each other joyfully. I saw the procession fifteen months after I had lost my own son and understood a little of the heart-cleansing that Aristotle talked about, the catharsis through pity and terror, though the pain was still there, my new and unwanted life companion. But the Madonna wears green under her black robes, the color of new life, the symbol of hope. Maybe what was under Ma's need for drama was always the need for hope.

Maria Domenica stares into the camera, unsmiling, inky eyes wide, hair a kinky fright wig standing straight up like a crown of thorns, her misery palpable. Her expression is the same I have seen on the faces in daguerreotypes of slaves. She looks stunned by pain, disassociated from the world. This tinted picture is all I know of my grandmother, along with my mother's spare, cryptic tales of an unhappy marriage and a bullying spouse. I picture the screams, the cracked-whip slapping sounds, my mother running through the dark night, the peak of the Gran Sasso looming over her like a judgment, her terror of wolves almost as great as the fear that her mother will be dead by the time she returns, murdered by her father. Six months after my mother emigrates, Maria Domenica dies at thirty-nine of a burst appendix, thus ending her short, unhappy life.

Ma's Father

I sit at the scarred oak table in my kitchen trying to decipher a tissue-thin fragment of a semiliterate letter dated 5/6/1941. I feel like a code breaker. Translating this isn't going to change the world, like the unraveling of the German Enigma code. This almost hopeless endeavor is only about time traveling and truth digging and searching for the *vero cuore*, the true heart of my grandfather, the person my mother reviled all her life. My grandfather is the man who tried to marry off my teenage mother to an old hunchbacked man with a lot of land for a dowry, like some implacable evil king in a fairy tale, the man who was responsible for my mother leaving Italy at eighteen and never seeing her mother again.

This letter is from my grandfather to my mother not long after she married my father. My mother had been in this country for five years and was twenty-three years old, by my reckoning. All I have to go on is this torn sheet of onionskin, crumpled and stained with inkblots and age. My mother usually tossed away written keepsakes with the same abandon that she threw chewed artichoke leaves into the swill bucket under the sink after a Sunday dinner.

Grade-school paintings, my middle school diaries, baby books, Mother's Day cards—Ma cared nothing for memories made of paper, it seemed. But she kept my father's wartime letters to her from the time when they were newlyweds until she died. Her father's letter was stuffed carelessly in with those far more treasured pieces of her heart.

The letter before me now is in Italian, in an unfathomable Abruzzese dialect. I can pick out one or two words easily; the phrase that leaps out is *"vero cuore"*—true heart—near the end of the letter. As to the body of the letter, I am at the mercy of my Italian-English dictionary, which is only marginally helpful because of all the misspellings, the dialect, the baroque handwriting, and the torn paper. I can surmise that Ma sent him a photograph, probably of herself and my father, because my grandfather later refers to her husband as a *bel ciovanoto*—a misspelling of *giovanotto*—a handsome young man.

I know that in May of 1941, Italy was under the spell of Il Duce and allied with Nazi Germany, and that Italy had invaded Ethiopia and Greece. My grandfather was a small farmer and a fascist, also mesmerized by Mussolini's wild promises of conquest and glory. I know that my grandfather had remarried only six months after my grandmother died, perhaps because Il Duce had promised a bounty for sons. My mother never forgave him for this second marriage, and the disgrace of not giving her mother a full year of mourning. I know that my grandfather had in 1941 two young daughters and no sons, a fact that probably made my mother perversely happy.

I have a picture of my grandfather in Sulmona, from when I visited there in 2006. It is the only picture of him that exists. I know this because during that same visit I asked my mother's half-sister, Domenica, in my halting Italian, if there were any pictures of her father. She nodded, left the room, and returned with a rifle. I took a picture of my aunt holding it, since this was all she had that belonged to her father, a gun. I missed my mother, thinking of that gun, and pictured how she would've snorted at the significance of a gun as his metaphor, even though she wouldn't have put it that way. In the midst of that absurdity, I was moved by my aunt's sweet earnestness as she thrust the gun toward me, across a universe of misapprehension. But there was an image of my grandfather at the cemetery. In the oval picture mounted on his tomb, Ma's father is unsmiling, his mouth a thin line, a sturdy, fair-haired, light-eyed man who doesn't look older than fifty. There is no resemblance to my dark-haired, dark-eyed mother. I took a picture of the one on his grave, but my grandfather remained as opaque to me as the blurry oval on his tomb.

The few words I can translate from the slanting, crowded letters on the page before me mention his wife and Ma's grandparents. Twice he writes that he is happy that Ma is married to such a handsome man. He uses a word that means "clear things up" twice. I am curious if that refers to the bitterness that happened when Ma left for America against his wishes. I wonder if he is asking for help, or money, or for my mother to sign away her claim to the farm, a plea couched in many flowery *cara figlia* (dear daughter) expressions to cover the true heart of this letter.

My frustration and curiosity lead me to my good friend Patrizia. I sit in the comfortable chair at the superb restaurant that bears her name on a sunny afternoon in the quiet hours before the dinner rush. Patrizia is from Emilia Romagna in Italy but grew up in the south, in the city of Naples. She has graciously agreed to apply her skills to the letter before her on the table. "This is an antiquated version of Italian," she cries on first viewing. "So ornate and grandiose," she adds. She returns her attention to the letter, brows knit in concentration. I regard Patrizia as a sibyl and am a little in awe of her because she holds a law degree as an *avvocato* and is also a brilliant chef. I sip her dark, dark coffee, waiting for Patrizia's revelations to reanimate my grandfather.

It turns out that my halting Italian translation was correct—he wants my mother to get a "power of attorney" for seven hundred lire to release her grandmother's "stuff" that was left to my mother and her two half-sisters. Her father also says, plaintively, that he has written her another letter because he has heard that she "remarried a nice young man," but that no return mail has arrived. *"Remarried."* The casual way he uses the word—does that mean he bears no ill will for the way my mother left? There must certainly have been secret plans and whispered conversations. Does this one word mean forgiveness? Forgiveness for my mother crossing his will, disobeying his order? So many scenarios race through my mind: my grandmother facing his wrath alone after my mother's escape, the consequences, both physical and psychic for her deception. My mother, alone and afraid, on the train to Rome, then Naples, finding her way to the crowded docks in that pulsating, vibrant city of crime and passion.

Patrizia looks puzzled; this is because the letter, when folded, doesn't follow the way it should: first page, next page on the back of that one, then another page where he signs off, but on the back of that page, another spate of writing. She understands as she translates aloud to me: the added part is because when he went to mail the letter, he found one waiting for him from my mother. So he writes on the back of the letter he was about to send, saving paper. On the additional page my grandfather tells my mother that he was "so touched and happy to receive your photos and you are so beautiful and you have married a handsome young man that I like a lot." He instructs my mother to give my father his best regards and gives her fatherly advice, to love her husband and to "allow me to love you as your parent." He warns her to "be careful and show respect, and to at least be happy in life because life goes by—be happy, otherwise the people laugh at you." Patrizia notes that the handwriting, though ornate, is labored. I picture his calloused farmer hand dragging across the thin paper, tearing it before it is sent, and his aggravation at himself for presenting a *brutta figura*.

"Otherwise the people laugh at you." A man of rages who fears being laughed at more than death itself. The bully's hallmark.

My grandfather's closing words to my mother are the ones that finally move me. Like my mother has done in writing a birthday card to me, he signs his full name. This is the way illiterate people who are not used to putting their signature on anything but official papers sign their names, last name first, like they are mustering for the army or selling a cow. "With a true heart, I inscribe: your affectionate father, Leombruno Gaetano. *Adio* [misspelled] write soon and good news." And then, trailing at the bottom of the last page like a dying bird, another misspelled and sorrowful "*Adio*," hanging alone and aslant in its own empty space.

Adio.

Farewell.

Ma Gets the Last Word

"Don't say 'fuck' to the Coopers." I gripped Ma by both elbows and looked into her eyes. I was nervous. She shrugged me away, irritated, and headed back to her kitchen domain to produce one of her classic dinners. My newly acquired, upright-citizen in-laws were in town from Kansas City and about to meet my family for the first time, even though my husband and I had been married for two years. I was on a random visit home when my mother-in-law phoned to say that she and my father-in-law were at Massachusetts Eye and Ear to deal with his detached retina. My husband, Chris, was in London performing in a Tennessee Williams play directed by Harold Pinter, but that oddball juxtaposition was not as bizarre as the one about to happen in my childhood home.

The Leones and the Coopers had never met because Chris and I had eloped, if that's what you call it when you live together for five years and decide to avoid future bureaucratic hassles by legalizing the situation in as low key a way as humanly possible. That meant telling both sides of your family that you had summer stock in a few weeks and no time for an elaborate wedding.

Now my husband was getting to act with Lauren Bacall in London, and I was left to wrangle the relatives meeting for the first time ever across a chasm as wide and mysterious as the Sargasso Sea. When I wasn't considering and discarding various revenge scenarios for Chris in my head, I was stamping down my teenage id-fear and shame demons that had arisen from the place kept at bay by my newfound happiness with Chris. I had met my in-laws before this impromptu visit to our house and we had spent our first Christmas as husband and wife with them. When we drove up to their home, I suddenly channeled my mother. I turned to him, and said, "What the fuck, Chris (*"che cazze!"*)! You didn't tell me you lived in a national monument!" Chris laughed it off and tried to assure me that his mother had snatched up the house at a bargain-basement price, but I was intimidated by the looming three-story Southern colonial mansion sitting in front of a fountain on a grand boulevard, whose white crenulated pillars stood like a phalanx of bodyguards already deeming me unworthy to cross the threshold. Once inside, I found myself reverting to my trisyllabic-word posture, the shield from my uncertain teen years. "Let's go into the library," Chris's mother said, her Texas accent turning "library" into "lahbrayrey." "How . . . magnanimous," I stuttered, noting with fleeting terror the spaghetti sauce bubbling on the stove as we passed quickly through the tiny kitchen. We wound our way through the stately dining room, past the grand staircase, through a Versailles-like living room, and into the library. "Take pitchas" my family suggested when I described the house to them later that night. I wondered how Chris's mother would react to my documenting her house like an insurance adjuster after a flood.

I was right to be terrified of the tomato sauce, as it turned out. My jaw dropped as I watched Chris's mother boil the pasta *in* the sauce. And it kept coming back, like a vampire's dregs, for three consecutive nights. My mother-in-law added some ketchup to the thankfully near-depleted sauce on the last night it appeared on the menu. I honed my acting skills to new heights and later lay in bed with Chris, stomach growling. On Christmas Eve, when my family was having *La Vigilia*, a seven-course feast featuring *pasta alla vongole*, stuffed calamari, shrimp, and cod, my family called Kansas City. "Whatta *they* havin'?" my aunt Ellie asked, grabbing the phone from my mother. I was too depressed to answer. "Mom, Marianne wants your recipe for the Jello mold," Chris said, after I hung up. He quirked his eyebrows at me and smiled his most devilish grin. "Muricle Whip," she answered. I stared at the green alien glob quivering before me and prayed for release.

By the time my in-laws arrived at Ma's house, I was twitching and clearing my throat with a tic-like regularity not seen since my days as a first-grader terrified by the yawning gates of hell.

Social awkwardness, pungent as my mother's tomato sauce, permeated the air around the dinner table. My aunt Sara and uncle Joe sat side by side, mute, corpse-like smiles plastered on their faces. Upon my in-laws' arrival my mother had groveled, salaaming before my mother-in-law's tall blond all-American good looks. "You so beautiful," she crooned, like a plainsong chant of appeasement. The other Mrs. Cooper, Mary Ann (yes, we have the same name), beamed with noblesse oblige. I thought of the stately portrait of Mary Ann in a celestial blue gown gracing her formal dining room, as if to distract from the food served there. My own family's arts and crafts dining room looked kitschy and cramped. But the food was spectacular. I watched my handsome father-in-law eating his lasagna with relish. We got through the dinner, I thought with relief, as the meal wound to a close. But while I made coffee in the kitchen I heard my mother's voice from the other room, loud and defiant. I got back in time for the raised finger jab, punctuating the barked "No!" She looked fierce, like she was channeling Anna Magnani via Benito Mussolini.

"When I wanna die, I die."

"Now, Linda, you can't just—" came the aggrieved voice of my father-in-law, cut short by another, more decisive "No" from Ma.

At the end of the day, Ma won the argument on euthanasia by sheer force of will—"When I wanna die, I die" was her coup de grâce, delivered with the force of a karate punch to the throat. But she never once said "fuck" to the Coopers. Chris's mother deemed Ma a "spitfire," and my mother's only remark about her (sotto voce, when she was out of earshot) was

"Yeah, she look nice but don' cross 'er, right?"

(An astute observation, as it turned out.)

Ma Picks a Priest

"I rest my case,"

My sister, Lindy, thrust a statue of Saint Anthony in my face, tick-tocking him like a metronome. Saint Anthony was wearing a rakish pink scrunchie around his waist, stuffed with red and yellow artificial flowers. We were arguing about holy cards and which saint Ma would want on hers. I had pushed Saint Rocco in honor of Ma's part-time job booking illegal numbers for the local wise guys. I thought I remembered her telling me that Saint Rocco was the patron saint of gambling. He was often depicted as a ragged man with bleeding leg sores being licked by a faithful dog. (I later found out that he was invoked to ward off infectious diseases.) I supported my vote for Saint Rocco with the fact that Ma had a statue of him right by her bed. My sister pointed out that Saint Anthony was there, too. So was Saint Jude, a flame shooting out of his head like he had just been electrocuted, and Saint Francis, decked out like a mad pigeon lady in Central Park with birds clinging all over his monk's robes, even covering his privates. But Saint Anthony had the scrunchie with the flowers. And Ma had put it there herself.

"Look at him. He's *decorated*," my sister said.

We both cracked up. Then we cried. Again.

We had been on an emotional roller coaster for two days now, ever since Ma died suddenly at the age of eighty-four. The doctors said it was a cerebral hemorrhage. She woke up with a headache and was dead by two the same afternoon. Ma would've liked the idea of leaving in such a hurry, like one of our childhood Christmas trees that was stripped and tossed every year the day after Christmas, at her urgent behest.

Now my brother, Michael; Lindy; and I were orchestrating the wake and funeral, checking off chores with the same haste as we used to devour desserts, Ma waiting impatiently to clear the dinner table. Apart from the quibble about her favorite saint, we knew exactly what to do. From birth to marriage to death, there was a clear trajectory if you lived in the Lake, where the circle of life had a really tiny radius. You were baptized at Our Lady Help of Christians Church, you got your wedding dress at La Sposa, you were laid out across the street at Magni's Funeral Home, and your funeral Mass send-off returned you to Our Lady Help of Christians Church.

No matter that Ma never went to church except for weddings or funerals, no matter that Ma couldn't name who was the monsignor of Our Lady's, nor the name of the current pope, she wanted the grand send-off with every available rite and that included her coffin carried down the main aisle of the church to rest before the high marble altar. She wanted organ music and eulogies and tears, as befitted her years on this planet, and you couldn't get that anywhere else.

Andrew Magni led us through the downstairs coffin display. We bypassed the over-the-top one with the carved version of the Last Supper on the cover, paused briefly by the hot pink number so my sister and I could instant eyebrow message each other, and settled finally on a shiny metal canister with a coppery glint. Back in his office, Andrew informed us that none of the regular priests at Our Lady's were available and we would have a substitute from the next parish over, Saint Bernard's, to say Ma's funeral Mass. The name of the parish rang a tiny, distant bell muffled by my memory of Ma's last non-encounter with priests a few months before she died.

We were at Newton-Wellesley Hospital. Ma had complained of a headache and partial loss of vision in one eye, and the doctors wanted to make sure she hadn't had a small stroke. I stayed with her so that her spotty English-language skills wouldn't make her seem unhinged to the medical staff; they were testing her mental competence with questions about what day it was, what month, and what year. She answered correctly. They asked her who was the current president that year, 2004.

"Eh. I ken' remember his name, but I know he's a *basta'*!"

I looked at the hospital personnel.

"You can't possibly question her sanity now."

Nevertheless, the doctors decided to keep Ma overnight. They sent in a very young, squeaky-voiced hospital clerk, who rattled off a list of questions in a fatally bored voice.

"Religious affiliation?"

Ma looked at me and shrugged.

"What's 'e want?"

"He wants to know if you want to see a priest."

Ma's voice was strong, resolute.

"No. No priest."

I turned to Squeaky.

"You got that? No priests."

Squeaky didn't realize that to my mother it was as if he'd asked: "And would you like to have a visit from the Angel of Death?"

Later, I settled Ma in her intensive care room—there were no beds available in the regular part of the hospital. She relaxed, lulled by the electronic wallpaper of the television mounted in the corner. Restless, I wandered into the hall. I stopped at the cubicle next door, arrested by the sound as a priest droned the Our Father to a frightened, demented old woman who was emitting cries of alarm like a baby bird dislodged from the nest. I edged closer. "Home. Home," the old woman cried. She lay huddled on her bed in a wilted heap, barely distinguishable from the bedclothes. The priest sat four feet away and recited his prayer as if he were alone in the room, as if he were direct-dialing his old buddy God for a dinner date, as if the old woman were already dead.

Ma was right about priests, I thought.

About a month after the hospital event, I was on a flight from Los Angeles heading home to Boston. We were in first class, courtesy of the studio that was promoting Chris's film. I sat beside an entitled middle-aged guy who wasn't about to give up his window seat so I could sit with Chris. That was okay. Chris and I could survive five hours one row apart. And we were in first class. Who was I to complain when there were warm cookies available and I had actual legroom? Just six rows back in the economy gulag there were cramped throngs with serious future chiropractor bills looming and no warm cookies. I didn't hold it against the window-hugging guy and over lunch we made polite small talk. I asked him why he had been to LA. He said he was at a religious convention.

"Oh, really? What do you do?" I asked brightly, with only a tinge of heart-sink at the word "religious." I knew that my own contentious nature and the twelve years I put in as a parochial school POW would inexorably draw me into talking about religion. I was a lemming in sight of the cliff.

"I'm a priest," he said, with a kind of mock sheepishness, like he was revealing unwillingly his superpowers.

I leapt off the cliff.

"I hope you don't think you're more spiritual than I am because you have a penis and can change water into wine."

That came out so abruptly I almost looked around to see who said it.

The priest raised his arm for the stewardess like he was bestowing a blessing.

"I'll have a scotch, please."

Over the next five hours we discussed my theory of the imminent demise of the Catholic Church. Well, I scattershot bullet points at the priest, and he dodged them. It was strange. I remembered the worshipful way the nuns would ask the priests if they would give us a blessing back in high school when they visited our classrooms. The nuns would duck their heads girlishly and we students fell obediently to our knees in a thudding horde. They had glamour then, the priests. They handled God every day. A tiny, retro part of myself wanted the God spillover from the guy sitting next to me in the window seat. But I also wanted him to explain to me why any woman would want to join a club that from birth designated her as a second-class citizen. He talked about the programs he was involved in for troubled youth. I talked about the Magdalene laundries in Ireland, the Catholic-run slave-labor institutions for unwed mothers that only closed in the nineties. I asked if his youth programs were like that. He kept ordering scotches. Even though he was the one drinking scotch, my memory of the rest of the discussion is hazy, though I know it touched upon my years of torment in parochial school, the priest pedophile scandals, and my gratitude to Renaissance cardinals for commissioning 3-D pornography from artists like Bernini so that we could today view Italian sculptures of women in "spiritual" ecstasy, like Santa Ludovica and Teresa of Avila.

Those once-lustful women carved of stone made me think of Ma, her fierceness stilled forever, on display in her burnished copper casket. I remembered asking her on New Year's Day what her resolution was for 2004, and her growly answer: "to be dead this year." And then her practiced hold for my laugh, her timing as polished as any late-night comedian's. Her pitch-black humor, which had taken seed in the arid mountain soil of her impoverished girlhood, was as gnarled and twisted as the Montepulciano grape arbors of that region, and as dry and delicious as the dark wine they produced. I don't remember ever hearing a belly laugh from Ma. She favored the snort of derision, the head toss, the "ha!" that was

more like a spoken confirmation that she got the joke. As mea-
sured as her own laughter was, she was sly about amusing her audience. She knew she was funny but she always played it straight.
She acted the innocent, watching us laugh, eyelids at half-mast,
appraising the reactions. Ma would never make me laugh again,
I thought.

On the day of Ma's funeral, I entered the church just as the
substitute priest was setting up shop for the requiem Mass he
was about to say. I squinted at the altar. I put on my glasses and
looked again.

It was my scotch-drinking seatmate from the plane. I snorted
with laughter, my laugh a replica of my mother's.

Ma and the Afterlife

Ma didn't believe in the afterlife, not the eternal hell and its varied torments so vividly described by the nuns, nor the good-cop version from the same religious overlords, the candy-colored heaven pimped out as her final reward if she would only behave and follow their rules.

Even if there was no afterlife, as she claimed, Ma was coming to me in various forms from somewhere after she died. Maybe it was only the long echo of her life on Earth reverberating in my own head. How else to explain that bark in my ear, the distinct sound of her growly voice saying my name in her singular way that sounded like "MUDDY-AHN!" No one else said my name like that. What did she want? What was so urgent that compelled her spirit, or my imagining of her spirit, to yell so obscenely early one morning that I leapt from my bed, disoriented, time-traveling back to panic-thinking I was late for school? There was no urgency to her clarion call, no attempt from the beyond to save me and my family from fire or burglars or other calamities that I could report to a reality-TV producer for a possible fifteen minutes of fame. Whatever the reason, it was definitely her voice, her unique, low-toned, gruff voice that always held a cry-laugh embedded in its signature sound. And as there was no earthly reason to yell in my ear, I can only assume it was sheer otherworldly mischief on Ma's part, an echo of the childish part of her that liked to poke hornet's nests, then stand back and claim innocence when the screaming began. Or maybe it was a last tiny gift, the first note of the comic or tragic aria she used to deliver every time we spoke, depending on her mood. I missed the daily installments of the Ma radio hour, the family gossip, the neighborhood death tallies, the consoling, smothering ever-present worry about me and my husband and child.

On the one-month anniversary of the day she died, Ma sent a random older man to me in the pasta section at Trader Joe's. As I pawed through the organic penne, trying to decide how many one-pound bags I needed, I felt someone's eyes on me. I looked up to see a pleasant-looking man staring at me, a beatific smile cracking the wrinkles on his Santa face.

"Your mother must be a beautiful woman," he said.

I stared back at him, not comprehending. He turned and wafted down the aisle, vaporizing almost as quickly as the cool mist surrounding the frozen pork *shu mai*. By the time I realized he was complimenting me through my mother, it also dawned that Ma was commemorating her own one-month anniversary by reminding me that she was once on Earth, that she was once considered good looking, and if a random guy thought I was, too, well, that was because of her.

Or—and this was a distinct possibility—I could also be approaching the age where I was geezer bait. Ma could be reminding me of that, too.

After Ma had been dead for some months I asked my sister if I could have the drawing of our mother that had hung in the same place on the parlor wall for as long as I could remember. My sister said she would bring it to me that weekend. I had always loved that charcoal drawing; the child snob in me believed that the portrait made our family seem genteel, like rich people who had art on their walls. It's clear looking at the picture through adult eyes that the sketch was probably something dashed off for fun on a night out at a carnival or on a boardwalk. The drawing has a plain black frame and is a broad-stroke rendering of my mother's strong features and thick raven's-wing hair. She is older here than in her twenties because she radiates a kind of confidence and strength that is missing from her earlier shy, almost sheepish demeanor in photographs as a newlywed on her honeymoon or posing awkwardly at the beach. As a child, I was entranced with the generic fifties' look of the portrait that softened Ma's Mediterranean features into an American blur. On our parlor wall she looked like she could be a Midwestern housewife pushing a vacuum cleaner in a graphic from the *Ladies' Home Journal,* like someone even-tempered and bland. Ma seems happy in the portrait, looking at life head-on, years away from the bitter, depressed persona who emerged when my father died. If the portrait had been drawn then, it would have shown an aura as dark as the mournful elegy from her *paese, scura mai,* dark forevermore.

The next morning after we agreed to transfer the portrait to my house, my sister called, shaken. The charcoal portrait had jerked her awake when it crashed to the floor in the deep gloom before dawn.

"I got scared," my sister said, laughter jiggling the word "scared" into the two-syllable squeaky register of a child spooked by night terrors. A vivid picture arose of my five-year-old little sister sucking her thumb and fingering her undershirt for comfort. I felt like I had to reassure her. And myself.

"She was always impatient," I said.

"Still, it's weird," my sister insisted.

"I know," I said. A pause, while we both contemplated whatever force had hurled the portrait to the floor after so many years.

"Well, if she crashes off the wall here, we'll know she wants to go to Michael."

Michael is the only boy, the family hope, the *principe*, but he was a benevolent sun god and never used for evil on either of us the awesome power he wielded during our upbringing as most-loved child. My sister and I still made peevish jokes about which of us Ma would rescue if we all went down in a boat. (Hint: It would be the *masculine child*, in the words of Luca Brasi to Don Corleone on his daughter's wedding day.)

Ma has been on my wall for almost ten years now, bracketed cozily by other relatives, secure in her new space.

Not counting dreams, which may or may not be visits, Ma's messages from the afterlife have dwindled down to nothing in recent years. This gets me pondering if she's lost interest, become unconscious and subsumed into the cosmic goop, or, perhaps, like an actor sick of playing the same character type over and over, moved on to another role, another family, another life. If so, I get it; I really do. In my acting life, I seem to specialize in playing bitter, alcoholic mothers. Or nuns. I've played a lot of nuns. I get bored with the nuns and never the bitter alcoholics—but that's my own karmic story. I hope Ma's story continues somewhere, somehow, and that she never yells in my ear again.

Everybody's Dead

When I am about six I rescue a baby bird I find under the apple tree. The bird is so new there are no feathers and it looks like a baby dinosaur. It lies still and unmoving in my hand. It is not asleep. It looks like it is dead. I bring it into our cellar and place it carefully next to the furnace. I believe that the heat will bring the bird back to life. I am learning in school about Jesus coming back to life—after three days! I know from the Disney movie *Peter Pan* that Tinkerbell was revived by the clapping of hands and the audience's fervent belief in fairies. Faith brought her back to life. But the bird is dead, no matter what I do or how deeply I believe in birds. I know now that death is final and cannot be deterred by faith.

I am hard-wired for morbidity and addicted to death. I blame this on my Italian DNA, on the *fatalismo* that flows through my veins, a Stygian artery that ferries the inevitable gloom to its final destination in my dark heart. I want to be American and optimistic; instead I obsess about mass extinctions and regard a pregnant woman with sorrow, thinking of the post-apocalyptic nightmare

in which her feral children will probably roam the earth, scrabbling for food in the devastated hellscape that awaits us all. I think
that I don't want to reincarnate. If reincarnation is real, I want to
be flung off the karmic wheel after this one, please. Maybe I'm
descended from the Trausi tribe that Herodotus wrote about. He
said in his *Histories*, "When a child is born all its kindred sit round
about it in a circle and weep for the woes it will have to undergo
now that it is come into the world." I bet if I sent away for a DNA
test it would come back 60 percent Trausi.

If I am specific, I can narrow down the blame for the genetic
obsession with gloom. It comes directly from my mother, flowing down from her DNA to mine like the mountain waters that
once coursed through the two-thousand-year-old aqueduct in her
hometown of Sulmona. Ma was the model for the original Goth
Girl. She was never girlish, but she nailed ghoulish before it was
cool. She kept a stack of plastic cards by her easy chair in front of
the television. They were memento mori, emblazoned with saints
and religious imagery on the front and the names of the dead
on the back. Ma shuffled through them like a cardsharp in some
movie western, cataloguing the dead, over and over. Her fascinated
grandchildren were as familiar with lurid pictures of a bleeding
heart encircled by a crown of thorns as they were with the charming reproductions of Beatrice Potter in their nighttime storybooks.

"I ken' cry! I ken' *cry*, Muddy-Ahn!" my mother wailed to me
over the phone one day. This was a serious situation. My mother
wept daily over tragedies from domestic disturbances like dropped
eggs to world events like tsunamis. It turned out her emotions
had become flat-lined due to an antidepressant prescribed by her
doctor, a kindly Asian gentleman who was respectful of his elderly
clientele. I could envision what had transpired in his office visit
with Ma. He had asked how everything was and my mother had
shrugged, sighed, and told him "everybody's dead," summoning
the mournfulness of an entire Greek chorus in just two economi-
cal words. I called the doctor and explained that he should consult

one of her daughters before prescribing any more antidepressants for our mother. His polite manner kept me from expressing my real suspicion that Ma was prescribed one of the "shut the fuck up and stop complaining, old person" drugs that are given out like after-dinner mints in doctors' offices all over the country whenever an elderly person mistakes a question about themselves as an actual inquiry expecting a real answer about their lives. "Everybody's dead" is a perfectly legitimate answer to describe what's going on in your eighties. Pretty much everybody you hung around with in your twenties *is* dead. And instead of sedating Ma into compliance, the pills had now made her more upset that she had no release for her sadness about the disappearance of old friends, family, shopkeepers, people in the nightly news—everybody that's dead. Or about to be dead. Everybody.

I get it. There are days when I look at my two little bichons, now rapidly approaching senior citizen status, and wonder which of them will die first, then ponder how I will get the survivor to walk without his partner. An upbeat, glass-half-full person would look at them prancing in the yard and think how far they've come from the horrendous abuses of the puppy mill from which they were rescued. They would marvel at their resilience and renewed trust in humans. Instead, I hear Ma's voice ricocheting off my own darkness, picturing what she would say as she stares dolefully at my dogs, snuggled together on the chaise, basking in the sun: "Eh, *poverelli*. Poor things. Looka that fat one. He remind me of the little pig I 'ad. I loved that pig. (Long, dolorous pause) They made 'im into salami."

When my friend Maureen's mother died, she came to my house to drop off her son while she made funeral arrangements. My mother was visiting for the weekend. Maureen sat at the table, stunned and silent in the first hours of an inevitable and fully expected death. Mossie, Maureen's Irish mother, had been a longtime favorite of mine. I remembered her big whoop of a laugh and her love and devotion to her daughters, Maureen and Katy, not to mention the hours she spent around the kitchen table with us as teenagers, cadging cigarettes and giggling over our silly pranks. Mossie had even chauffeured us around town when we were bored preteens, so we could scope out cute boys and squeal in the back seat of her roomy old Chevy. She had been ailing these last years after a devastating stroke robbed her of her lovely Cork brogue and room-filling laughter. Ma sat across from Maureen at our round oak table, regarding her dejectedly.

"You mother's lucky, Maureen. I wish *I* was dead," she offered by way of consolation.

Maureen told me later that every time she thought of Ma's special condolences, she laughed. In that sense, Ma was a medium, of sorts, channeling Mossie for one last time and using her special talent to make her daughter laugh again. But Ma usually functioned more as a bell-ringer, as in "Bring out your dead."

Some examples:

I am sitting beside my mother during my brother's wedding ceremony. Suddenly, she groans and clutches my arm during his vows as if she were taking back his birth. Later, she tells me: "I felt like 'e was drowning, like 'e was gonna die and I couldn't save 'im."

My husband and I are at my mother's house for Christmas. We have told her that Chris's father has cancer, so when carolers serenade us outside, my mother goes out to tell the joyful Noel-ers that someone related to someone in the house is dying. Even though my husband's father is a thousand miles away. And his death isn't really imminent.

And then this one, the real jaw-dropper in what is an only partial list of Ma's death announcements: On the day of my son's birth, I called Ma to tell her that I had delivered my son ten weeks early. I reported to Ma that he was born alive, without drugs, and was doing all right so far. I was still shaken from delivering so soon, but optimistic about my son's chances for survival. An hour or so later, I dialed my aunt Ellie's number from my hospital room. She gasped when she heard my voice. "Your mother said you were *dead*," she said. "Dead?" I asked. Even for Ma, this was a new level of Greek tragedy. "Well, she said you were bad," Ellie replied, adjusting to the horror in my voice. "Really, really bad. Almost dead. She said—" and here I stopped listening or trying to figure it out.

I recognized the impulse. It was as familiar to me as the sight of my mother's gnarled hands forking the anti-*malocchia* sign to ward off evil. If you pictured the worst thing that could happen, maybe it wouldn't. If you said it aloud, maybe it would create a circle of protection just by giving it voice.

That must be why, I reasoned later, after life as I knew it came to an end, my mother had no words when she came to me in a dream after her death. She returned again and again on different nights, always dressed in white, always silent, always symbolically arrayed beside a table with a lone candle burning, a riddle I couldn't decode. Why was she so forbidding, so austere? Why didn't she speak? What was she trying to say?

There were no words when I found my seventeen-year-old son dead, only the high-pitched, brain-piercing sound of the universe ending.

There were no words when four months later, my aunt Ellie died. No words when eleven months later, Uncle Benny died. When Goody, Jesse's dog died, the deathly procession came to an end, and then everybody was dead.

Frozen

We glided into the pale-blue viewing room in the dream state that makes movement watery and slow. My little niece, living in real time, ran to the coffin and kissed our mother's waxen effigy. "Mumma!" she shouted, turning to my sister, her reedy voice astonished, her face alive with wonder: "She's like a popsicle!" The fixed smirk on our mother's face didn't break into a laugh, but I did, and was thus ejected from the dream. I knew that Ma had triggered the most vivacious child in our family to shake me back into this roiling life, to make sure I woke up and got the joke.

Epilogue
Ma's Hands

My aunt Ellie was the one who told me about seeing Ma put her fist through a door in a fit of rage. It seemed like an exaggerated story to me. Not that I didn't appreciate the drama and the casual way Ellie threw out the line, like she was baiting a hook. But I couldn't picture it. I'd seen my mother in rages but just how angry did you have to be to need that kind of contact? To risk damaging those fragile bones, ending up in a cast, encased in plaster for a month, immobilized? It was a mystery, like the stigmata the nuns were always talking about, the condition they considered blessed, when your hands bled in sympathy with the wounds of Christ. But Ma didn't seem blessed so much as someone composed of alien DNA. I had raised my own fist many times, marching in the streets against war or for reproductive rights. It was symbolic. It didn't involve a possible fracture or other form of self-immolation. Another Ma mystery I couldn't solve.

Louie, a distant relative in the way that everyone who lives in my old neighborhood is a distant relative, tells this story about Ma. One day Louie went into the kitchen of the restaurant where Ma worked on Adams Street. He watched her stirring the sauce. The thing is, as Louie tells it, she was stirring the simmering sauce *with her hand*. Of course, this apocryphal story relies on the say-so of a man who dresses as an elf every Christmas. A very large elf. I love hearing Ma mythologized in a tale like this. That it's a tale told by a grown man dressed as a character on a cookie box makes the story even more delightful.

Ma's hands did seem impervious to heat. She had chef's hands crisscrossed with cuts and burns, some of the burns drifting to her forearms and remaining there as battle scars of her years in the kitchen. My sister and I have observed our mother taking pans out of the stove without potholders, like some superhero strangely endowed with inflammable hands. Ma was blasé about her super-power and scoffed at the rest of us for being unwilling to expose ourselves to third-degree burns. Lindy and I did not inherit the gene for handling hot plates with no damage, however. Nor can I figure out why there would even be reason for such a gene. It was just another in the strange catalogue of facts about our mother.

My uncle Benny, Ma's brother-in-law, told me that he first met my mother rolling out Sunday's pasta dough. He said she was pregnant with me and he could never forget the sight of her leaning across the table, her awkward bulk pressing against the wooden pasta board, handling the dough with the strength of a prizefighter. Like a dancer displaying both power and grace, the same hands that punched and pummeled the dough into submission could also slice the rolled log of dough into thin strands of linguine with the precision and alacrity of a neurosurgeon separating the complex and winding threads of neural pathways.

———

Ma pets the long, silky christening dress on the baby doll she had laid out in its new crib, center stage on the dining room table. She waits for me to come home from school, hoping for a look of wonder, followed by gratitude, maybe even tears of joy. I see the doll and say nothing, shrinking away. I hate baby dolls. I thank her, barely, and go upstairs with my new library book. Her hands return to arranging the miniature baby in its crib. When I go back to school tomorrow, she will give it love.

My mother tosses the salad with her hands. Dinner is running late, my father will be home soon. I give out a full-body shudder, like someone in the grip of a malarial ague. I make retching sounds. Predictably, my mother snaps.

"Sominabitch!" she yells. Her angry face fills the room, a blood moon. "I chew the food and put in your mouth when you were a baby!"

I scream and laugh like a mad person, so revolted I feel almost euphoric. The brassy clanging of pots and pans accompanies the aria of curses as I run up the stairs to my room. Her oily, vinegary hand slaps the air, missing me.

Those veiny, ugly hands submerged in water, decapitating squid, oblivious to slime, flinging body parts into separate bowls, like a forensic pathologist, best pals with death. Those brutal hands, delicate now, waving her crochet hook in a silent incantation that creates spider-web lace out of thin air. Ma's hand lifted to her mouth sideways like a pirate's dagger, as she pretends to bite down, semaphoring the warning across a crowded room: "This hand could be you if you don't shut up and behave." The fingers of her hand twisting the meat of my upper arm in a pinch that is the sum of a full day's aggravation with me, and the fleshy substitute for the English words that fail to ever come at her command.

Ma's hands, calmer in old age, icing a cake for her granddaughter or guiding a straying toddler away from the cellar stairs.

Those brave and steady hands daring to feed my quadriplegic son.

Ma's hand, balled into a fist, shattering a door.

During the time we were fighting so that our disabled son could have the basic civil right to go to school with all the other kids, I bought a punching bag at a yard sale. I raised my fist, and, like before, it was a symbolic act, a stand-in for the deniers of my child's humanity, the eye-rollers, the false pitiers, the tiny-souled bureaucrats who had overtaken my life. It would have been a relief to actually punch a door, shattering my own bones and removing me from the war. But the actual punch wasn't as important as the ability to bend, not break, until the barrier was removed. A slow learner, I only figured this out after many symbolic blows to my own head. And I never saw how Ma had used her hands to bend, not break, when she was indeed a stranger in a strange land, an alien, not from another planet but from another culture—left adrift and unmoored with three kids, no skills, and a slippery grasp of the English language.

I take a tai chi chuan class twice a week. Today, the instructor told us a literal translation for the soft martial art: "supreme ultimate fist." I thought immediately of the weeping cherry tree planted in Ma's memory in our backyard. In a kind and generous gesture, two of our neighbors planted the tree on an uncommonly hot early spring day. At the time I thought of how much Ma would have appreciated the sight of two strong men in shorts sweating bullets on her behalf. But the reason I thought of Ma's memorial tree is the shape it invariably takes, despite yearly prunings. Ma's tree refuses to bow down and weep, the way it should. Instead the two branches at the top point to the sky, forming a fist.

A "supreme ultimate fist."

It has been eleven years since Ma's death. Her tree fist has unfurled like a riddle that is finally revealed. The branches of my mother's tree all weep together now, in unison. In the spring, though, they manifest the opposite of grief. Instead, a canopy of pink flowers cascades as one, swaying together like those men who bide their time, and then at some unknown signal, break into a joyful run every Easter morning carrying their Madonna toward a dream that is the embodiment of hope.

How I Think Ma Made Her "Meatless" Lentil Soup

This cobbled-together recipe is all guesswork. But I have tried it out and while it's not an exact replica of my mother's "meatless" lentil soup, it's pretty good. Unless you compare it with the original that Ma made. Or the identical twin *zuppa di lenticche* I found in that hole-in-the-wall *ristorante* in Napoli, the one that made me cry after tasting it. Those two are still the paradigm of all lentil soups, unattainable so far in my kitchen but something to strive for.

Ma didn't share recipes, and it took years, until I became an accomplished cook myself, before I finally realized she wasn't deliberately misleading me so she would retain her title as Queen of All Italian Cuisine. I was understandably suspicious of the way she would leave out key ingredients or amounts when I asked her how to make one of her signature dishes. Now I understand. A lot of what I cook is by feel, not numbers. A handful of this, a pinch of that. Ma cooked like that, too. That said, I apologize for anything in this guesswork recipe that isn't precise.

First, you need to make the hand-rolled and hand-cut pasta. You won't have to do any cardio workouts for the next few days if you do it right. My husband and I tried to get our dough as thin

as the pasta dough Ma turned out effortlessly every Sunday, and
we broke a sweat, still didn't achieve Ma-level dough thinness, and
wimpily gave up after settling on non-credit card thinness. Maybe
you can do better. *In bocca al lupo.*

PASTA

3 cups of white flour (or semolina if you can get it)—or you could
    do half flour–half semolina

3 eggs

1 tbs. olive oil

water

Flour a pasta board or a large flat area on your table. Make a mound
of the flour in the middle. Make a cavity in the mound of flour, so it
resembles Vesuvio. Break the eggs into the cavity. Add the olive oil.
Swirl the eggs, mixing them, then start to crumble the flour walls
into the eggs. Start kneading the dough. Add a little more flour if it's
too sticky. Add a little water if it's too dry. Smooth the dough into a
ball and place in a bowl covered by a damp dish towel, or *moppina* as
my mother called them. Let stand for about an hour.

For pasta-machine users (it won't taste the same, I'm warning
you), turn the machine to number five.

Now, for those of you attempting the Ma way to do this, the
upper-body-strength part is next: Take the dough and place again
on the floured board. Flatten the dough into a disc. Take your rolling pin (I favor a long, thin dowel) and begin rolling the dough flat.
Keep rolling and turning the dough. Strew flour as needed. Take
needed breaks and swig some *vino rosso* to keep up your strength.

When the dough is leathery and very thin, roll it into a log like a
jellyroll. Cut the noodles into linguine size lengths, then shake them
out and lay them to dry out on more dishtowels. (That is how Ma did
it, only she made it look like a magic trick. Maybe you can, too.)

I always have opera playing in the background. Ma usually
had Louis Prima. Or Dean Martin or Teresa Brewer. Whatever, it

somehow helps flavor everything for those of us who have succumbed to magical thinking. (But it works, I swear.)

THE "GRAVY" (TOMATO SAUCE)

About a two inch cube of salt pork
One medium onion, diced
Two or three cloves of diced garlic
Two cans of whole peeled San Marzano tomatoes
One can tomato paste, plus one can of water
Dried basil and oregano and just a pinch of mint
Boneless pork spare ribs (about one pound)
Olive oil
Red wine
Salt and pepper to taste

In a big soup pan, place the salt pork, and when it renders, add
pork ribs, diced onion, and minced garlic. Brown the pork for at
least twenty minutes, turning occasionally. Open cans of peeled
Italian tomatoes and place in food mill over pan (my mother used
a simple one with a hand-turned grinder). You could also just use a
food processor, but then you will have seeds. Up to you. Open can
of tomato paste and add to sauce, plus one can of water. Throw in a
dollop of red wine. Then later, after you've drunk some of the wine,
throw in some more. Grind some pepper into the sauce and add
some oregano and basil (I used a scant handful and my hands are
small—I think it would amount to about one tablespoon each) and
the pinch of dried mint. Simmer forever. About two hours at least,
stirring occasionally.

LENTILS

I don't think my mother had access to fancy-pants organic French
green lentils. I think she just used regular brown lentils she got at
Larry's Superette or my father brought home from Boston's North
End. If you are a food snob like I am, I totally understand you not

wanting to settle for plain old brown lentils. But I'm going for Proustian verisimilitude, so I'm using the brown. Feel free to go for the green. But remember to soak the lentils. If you do it overnight, you will reduce your cooking time by one hour. *Never* salt the lentils (this will make them tough).

OKAY, THE ACTUAL LENTIL SOUP

Two cups lentils
One medium onion, chopped
One tbs. olive oil
Chopped parsley, about ¼ cup
Two or three cloves of garlic, minced
One stalk celery, chopped fine
One carrot, peeled and chopped
Eight cups water
Two cups of the red sauce listed above
Hand cut noodles, listed above
Grated Romano, to taste

Again, use a big soup pan. Rinse and drain the lentils, picking out any stones. Add the olive oil to the pan and the chopped onion and minced garlic. Sauté until translucent. Add water, lentils, carrot, celery, and parsley. Bring to a boil and simmer for two hours. Add two cups of the tomato sauce.

Cook noodles separately and do not add until last minute.

Grate some Romano cheese before serving with a hearty red and crusty bread.

Make Ma's spirit happy by finishing your plate.

And *mille, mille grazie* to my friend Patrizia Galassi, proprietress of Patrizia's restaurant in Plymouth, Massachusetts, for her kind counsel. Patrizia, who grew up in Napoli, approved this recipe, and she is the kind of Italian chef you dream about having in your kitchen.

Acknowledgments

Mothers are always a mystery to their children, so I am immensely grateful to all who descended into the cavern with me to help decrypt these sibylline messages from Ma and shape them into a book that both decodes and celebrates her.

Thank you, Helene Atwan, for your wise and calm counsel and your knife-edge sharpness at solving puzzles.

Thank you, Colleen Mohyde, for seeing the book at the core of these disparate stories.

The design team at Beacon Press is outstanding and I am deeply grateful for their expertise in making this a beautiful book. Thank you to Bob Kosturko for an eye-popping cover and to Louis Roe for the gorgeous insert design.

Thanks to eagle-eyed Susan Lumenello for her painstaking copy-edits and to Marcy Barnes for her tireless work on the photo insert.

Grazie mille to Patrizia Galassi for helping me translate my grandfather's letter and for her invaluable aid in recreating my mother's lentil soup recipe.

Grazie mille to Edvige Giunta for illuminating the arcane secrets of my mother's dialect.

Thanks to early readers Mary Granfield and Tom Perrotta for their unflagging enthusiasm and encouragement, and to early listeners Fonni and Andre Dubus, who provided an appreciative and devoted audience for the stories that became the book.

My family, including my nieces and nephew, cousins, and extended family that is "the Lake," brought Ma back to me in little glinting anecdotes that helped me immeasurably.

And finally, thanks to my most trusted reader and listener, my husband, Chris, for whom Ma and I share a deep, burning love.